HEREWARD COLLEGE OF FURTHER EDUCATION
BRAMSTON CRESCENT
COVENTRY
CV4 9SW

This book is due for return on or before the last date shown below.

31. JUL. 1995		

Don Gresswell Ltd., London, N.21 Cat. No. 1208   DG 02242/71

WRITING
POPULAR
FICTION

To that renowned Editor, the late Harold Snoad,
and to his Literary Editor, the legendary Dorothy Sutherland,
whose combined faith in me – and encouragement –
led to my long career as an author.

WRITING POPULAR FICTION

Rona Randall

A & C Black · London

First published 1992
A & C Black (Publishers) Limited
35 Bedford Row, London WC1R 4JH

ISBN 0-7136-3568-1

A CIP catalogue record for this book
is available from the British Library.

Typeset by Florencetype Ltd, Kewstoke, Avon
Printed in Great Britain by Biddles Ltd.

Contents

1
The Way
to Authorship

Signposts and warnings

This book is written for people who want to become authors but don't know how to get started; for those who are already trying but are despairing; for those who have become discouraged by rejection; for those who have enrolled for tuition classes and drifted away either uninspired or deflated and believing that the fault lies in themselves, that they were never 'meant' to be authors; for those who, conversely, think they have only to attend creative writing courses for immediate publication to be guaranteed, and for those who have experienced a small measure of success, wish to advance further, but have somehow become stuck.

It is even written for those who imagine the job to be easy and a surefire way of making big money quickly. They have a lot to learn.

After spending virtually the whole of my adult life in non-stop professional authorship in a world of ever-changing public tastes, I believe aspiring authors can be helped to master the craft, but that it cannot be taught as some occupations are taught. Any branch of writing, and particularly fiction, is not a scientific or mathematical process which, once learned, will earn a string of letters after your name. Writing is a skill you will continue to learn for the whole of your life, but guidelines can act as signposts to set you on the right course and to keep you there.

The guidelines I present throughout this book should make the going less rough and steer you to success, providing you really want to achieve it.

I offer no magic formula, because there is none. In the final analysis it is you, the aspiring author, who wields the magic wand. Yours is the imagination, the love of words, the urge to create, the desire, the diligence, the dedication – and the self discipline. These are the tools you need; you must use them and never neglect them. My aim is to show you *how* to use them and to convince you that you *can* do it, even when hope seems at its lowest ebb.

There is one other vital tool which every aspiring author needs. Enthusiasm. Without it, no author's work will ever reach the popularity lists because enthusiasm is infectious; the reader catches it and awaits your next book eagerly. Thus a readership is built up and maintained. Lose that enthusiasm, and you will lose your readers and, in consequence, your publishers.

But that is not going to happen to you, because if you lacked enthusiasm you would not be reading this book.

Coupled with that essential quality is another to which few aspiring authors ever give a thought – self-honesty. By that I mean acknowledging the truth about your personal motivation. Ask yourself *why* you want to write. If your only answer is 'Money!' then you are not a born writer. Even if you sell some of your work you are unlikely to stay the course because when you discover that authorship is as unpredictable as any other form of self-employment, you will quit and seek a more stable job.

'But,' you argue, 'look at the gigantic sums paid to best-selling authors!'

Unhappily, that is as far as the general public does look because that is the only side to attract attention from the press. The steadily-selling authors who represent 90 per cent of the profession, and keep the library shelves filled, never achieve such publicity, but they would not abandon the work for any other because writing is the breath of life to them and, despite its demands on time and the sacrifice of much social life (five-day weeks are virtually unknown to full-time authors) they want no other career because this one gives the greatest self-satisfaction, which is what every real author writes for. Call it ego-gratification if you wish. He (or she) *must* write or mentally stifle.

The same applies to any branch of creativity. You have only to delve into the lives of past authors or artists or musicians to discover endless examples. What compelled Van Gogh or Gauguin to paint despite their sufferings, or Beethoven to compose when he could not hear a note of his music, or the Brontë sisters to write even when publication seemed an impossible dream? This passionate need for self-expression is in every writer who yearns to make authorship his or her career, no matter at what level – intellectual or non-intellectual.

This is not to say that money doesn't act as an impetus to output, but its value to writers is the freedom it brings to work in their own way, in their own time, at the job they most want to do. It is naturally exciting to hit the jackpot, but for many authors who achieve a steady, well paid and highly satisfactory living, jackpots are unknown. In my long years of authorship I have hit it only twice (and more colossal sums have since been paid for some colossal flops), but I have sometimes wondered whether I would have been spared a great deal of stress if it had never happened. The pressure to repeat the first success was too great to be enjoyable, and the mixture-as-before has never appealed to me. This raises the question of whether it is wiser to stay with one particular genre, or to diversify; to write various types of fiction under varying names, as many authors do, or to concentrate wholly on one. Once you are launched, the choice must be yours.

In my own case it so happened that, with the characteristic unpredictability of the publishing world, fashions in fiction suddenly changed and the popularity of the gothic, the genre in which I won this unexpected success, died abruptly, so I was glad I had followed my instinct and insisted on writing what I wanted to write. I stayed in the marketplace, but always under the same name.

It may be surprising to learn that fashions in reading matter can change. There can be various reasons for this. New television soap operas, setting new trends, can be one. Strong commercial hype by a publisher for a new type of story by a new name can be another. Or, as with the gothic, the market becomes flooded with badly written, badly constructed, and badly plotted imitations of currently popular fiction, launched by speculative publishers wanting to jump on the band waggon; the public's interest promptly takes a sharp fall and the market with it. When this happens, authors who confine themselves to one specific genre can be badly hit while those who turn to other types of fiction can survive if they have resolution and dedication. This only goes to prove that if your heart is wholly in it, nothing will deter you.

So if your true motivation is a passionate urge to write, let me welcome you to the fold. You will undoubtedly achieve your goal at whatever level you aim for.

If that aim is merely to entertain, it is equally laudable. In a world filled with increasing stress and pain and cruelty, what better occupation can there be than one which brings enjoyment to thousands of people? One of my greatest rewards came a year or two ago, mailed to me care of my publishers – an envelope with a Glasgow postmark containing a scrap of paper on which was written, very simply, 'Thank you for all the enjoyment your books have given me.' It bore no address and no signature, and accompanying it was a Scottish pound note. I have never parted with either. That kindly gesture has been kept as a talisman ever since. My only regret is that I have never been able to thank that unknown reader.

If, along the way, you experience a moment like that, you will know the joy of being an author.

Taking the first steps

There is a school of thought which insists that writers are born, not made; that no one can become a successful author by studying text books or attending creative writing classes; that every writer must be his or her own tutor, learning as they go (which means learning as they write and write and write). The parentheses are mine because I know that constant writing does indeed mean constant learning, but the rest I consider to be unduly sceptical. Not surprisingly, it comes mainly from the pseudo-intellectual, but it can destroy an aspiring author's confidence and a possible career. To such ill-formed opinion I urge you to turn a deaf ear, even though I am the first to concede that a totally unimaginative person would be more successful in another sphere (which they would be likely to seek anyway).

I am one who never attended creative writing classes, but I did have the advantage of four years on that long established monthly magazine, *Woman's Journal*, first as secretary to its distinguished editor, at that time one of the most prominent in London, then expanding into editorial work and journalism. During those years 'The Journal' was linked with three other publications, two women's weeklies and a highly regarded literary monthly called *Argosy* which featured only the best in short stories. Part of my training was in the field of fiction; learning what was required for the respective magazines, what was publishable and what was not, what readers would enjoy and what they would not (and why); reading submitted manuscripts, criticising them, reporting to an exacting fiction editor and facing the music if my judgment proved to be wrong.

I also sub-edited fiction, from short stories to serials, including the works of many established authors. This taught me the value of word economy and how judiciously to cut superfluous material. This was my training ground but, had I realised it, it was really my preparatory school. Searching for and editing publishable stories was a far cry from actually writing them. The toughest part came later; the slogging, stimulating, heart-breaking, challenging job of freelance authorship which, I quickly realised, is an entirely different skill from journalism or editing. Only then – writing, writing, writing – did my learning really begin.

The first salutory lesson was that authorship, like any creative work individually undertaken, is a lonely job. After the stimulation and team work of a busy editorial office, working in isolation demanded self-discipline. Domesticity and motherhood vied with, but were never threatened by, nostalgia for the environs of Fleet Street, at that time the heart of newspaper and magazine publishing, for I soon realised that freelancing offered the biggest plum of all – freedom to work in my own time, to be rid of commuting and its time-wasting hours, to combine writing with married life and so fulfil my ambition: to become an author. To anyone who shares that ambition, solitude is something to seize with gratitude. It is signpost number one, to be well heeded.

So if you are finding the going hard, just remember that I (and others) have been there, too. I know what you are going through. I have shared your hopes, your aspirations, your disappointments, your fears, your setbacks, your triumphs and disasters. All became mine when I struck out on my own. If *I* survived and conquered, you can, too.

And if creative writing classes and text books help you, as they can, don't listen to those who have no faith in them. In particular, don't listen to those (usually relations, but often so-called friends) who regard your writing as nothing but a hobby, and not much of a one at that. ('When are you going to look for a proper job? You'll never make money, scribbling!') Equally, don't pay too much heed, tempting as it may be, to those who say they have always known you were a born writer. Fulsome praise can be as damaging as derision, persuading you that any failure you experience must be the fault of others, never of yourself.

Conquering discouragement

I have great respect for tutors in the field of creative writing when it comes to discussing and dissecting writing techniques, but it is only when an author is alone with his pen and a stack of blank paper that his heart and his imagination will take over. If urged in a chosen direction by someone else, imagination can retreat, partly through self-consciousness but also through the fear of not matching up to a tutor's expectations or to the success of fellow students. And if the criticism of one's peers is involved, this sensitivity can be intensified. That is why I doubt the wisdom of students' efforts being read aloud in class, and when fellow aspirants are allowed to form a jury their verdict can be, at best, unreliable and, at worst, damaging.

I once witnessed a writers' circle meeting when competition entries were being read aloud and then voted on by members. Never having belonged to a writers' club, I was shocked to discover that such a practice was indulged in. They had been asked to write a story about a chair. Inevitably, there were stories about Grandfather's chair (all too obviously cribbed from the old nursery song about Grandfather's

clock), about antique chairs, rocking chairs, children's high chairs –
even an old kitchen chair which was actually supposed to be telling
what little story there was. Only one entry featured something different
– the electric chair, and the thoughts of a man condemned to it. It was
so well written that not until the end did one realise what kind of a chair
it was, or to where the man's journey of salvation was leading him.
Even more clever was the note of hope throughout the tale. It was
deeply moving and far from depressing. When it was unanimously
awarded the lowest marks of all, it was plain to me that the excellence
of the writing, the originality of the idea, the deep compassion, and the
skilful way in which it avoided any hint of despair were totally unappre-
ciated by the author's fellow members.

I asked to be introduced to the writer and was not surprised to find
her valiantly hiding her disappointment. Convinced that her story de-
served publication, I urged her to send it to one or two specific markets
and was delighted, but again not surprised, when her story was eventually published. Whether the winning entry ever was, a twee tale about
dear pussy's favourite chair, I very much doubt.

While it can sometimes be helpful to get an independent opinion on
a piece of work, and even more helpful if you can get a professional
one, I deplore the practice of exposing a beginner's work to the
criticism of other aspiring authors. Dorothea Brande, in her excellent
book *Becoming a Writer* includes a footnote for teachers in which she
condemns the practice as pernicious and an ordeal which can throw a
sensitive writer off his stride. She rightly stresses that when a beginner
is judged in such a way his or her critics 'seem to need to demonstrate
that although they are not yet writing quite perfectly themselves, they
are able to see all the flaws in a story which is read to them, and they
fall upon it tooth and fang'. I saw it happen that night.

Every aspiring author will grow at his own pace, in his own time and
in his own way, if his self-confidence is not undermined and even
destroyed (as it can be) by criticism from the wrong sources. Criticism
can and should be *con*structive, never *de*structive, as a writer will
discover when an editor begins to take an interest in his work and
suggests ways in which to improve it. That is part of an editor's job, and
to listen is part of a writer's.

Keep your own counsel

I strongly advocate the wisdom of never discussing your current piece
of work with anyone. I myself have erred in this way, and regretted it. In

one memorable instance when asked, by a fledgling author whom I had befriended, what the theme of my next novel was to be, I happily discussed it. I was about half way through the first draft, and enjoying it; a tale about the Owlers of Romney Marsh. She had never heard of that notorious gang of smugglers and enthusiastically asked for more, and more I foolishly revealed. I even outlined the basic plot, and was pleased by her appreciation of it. I even went a step further and introduced her to my agent. After that I never heard from her again.

Perhaps you have guessed the outcome, but I didn't even see it coming. She beat me to the post with a short and flimsy novel about the same notorious gang, with very familiar echoes, while my own book, a very much lengthier one, had still far to go.

I knew nothing of this until hers was in print, by which time *I* would have been the one to be accused of plagiarism had mine then appeared. Plagiarism is a serious offence and can land an author in trouble. I had no choice but to withdraw a script which represented well over a year's work, and ask my publisher to wait for my next. I had neither the desire nor the inclination to try to reshape my story, nor would it have worked well had I done so. My enthusiasm and my book had been killed stone dead.

Fortunately, incidents like that are rare. Far more frequent are those when an author, in response to a genuine interest from others, has begun to talk about his or her current work, only to find that in the telling it begins to sound flat and dull, particularly when the listener's attitude suggests it. Pamela Frankau's *Pen to Paper* offers a good example of this experience. She had the theme of her next novel 'safely tucked away in her head' after weeks of careful planning and even longer research, and went to a party feeling wildly happy because of it. Confiding the reason for her excitement to another guest, the woman immediately begged to hear all about it.

The author went ahead, only to find that with every word she spoke, it lost its magic; every character seemed cardboard, every situation weak and contrived, and the reaction of her listener spoke volumes. In talking about it, the book became stillborn.

These instances are quoted only in warning, to urge you to guard your precious ideas.

In contrast, you can take heart from Rhona Martin's experience with her first novel *Gallows Wedding*. Unwisely, the author discussed it with self-styled experts who promptly urged her to abandon it, declaring that it hadn't a hope of publication because it was 'too bloody, too earthy, and too violent' to fit into any category; 'too historical for a romance and too romantic for a historical'; that she was wasting her time in writing it. Obsessed with the story, she wrote it in secret and submitted it fully expecting rejection. It won the Bodley Head Historical Award in Memory of Georgette Heyer.

Didn't I say that it is when a writer is alone with pen, paper, and an urgent desire to write what he or she *wants* to write, that the best work comes?

My own experience with one of my most successful books, *Dragonmede*, was not dissimilar. Read by a former magazine serial editor who had switched to the very different sphere of book publishing, it was condemned by her on the grounds that there were too many characters and that the whole plot therefore needed drastic cutting and reshaping.

'Remember,' she wrote, 'that no full-length should have more than six characters . . .' and went on to suggest slashing out half the cast (including a murderer vital to the plot) and consequently eliminating half the action. I left her letter unanswered until, a month later, she wrote to enquire how far I had progressed with the 'very necessary reshaping', whereupon I sent her an outline of what would happen to the book were such alterations made, the whole thing falling apart.

I lacked the heart to tell her that she was viewing the novel in terms of a magazine serial, but from my own editorial experience I knew she was. Her very reference to a 'full length', an editorial term for serials as distinct from short stories, revealed that she had not left the magazine world behind her. This was also confirmed by her demand for only six characters, the convenient quota for serials because the limitations of instalments demand that the cast should appear month by month or week by week, the time lapse making it necessary for readers to be re-introduced to them. Too many characters in a serial therefore present problems.

I did venture to point out that a novel has a vast canvas with a matching scope for characterization; that characters can enter and exit and enter again without any need for re-introduction because the reader has the entire volume in hand. She was unconvinced, and replied that she would talk the whole thing over with me on her return from holiday. In her absence my agent's American counterpart sold the U.S. Volume Rights to a leading New York publisher, without a word being changed. It was made an Alternate Selection of the U.S. Literary Guild, an Exclusive Selection of the Doubleday Book Club, and the U.S. Paperback Rights were sold at auction for a jackpot figure. It also collected more Book Club selections in other countries, extensive sales of translation rights, and proved to be my most popular and profitable novel, worldwide, up to that date.

So take heart and don't give up hope. Your critics may not always be right.

But if you feel they are, even slightly, pay heed.

The author's greatest ally

It is not surprising that sensitive writers retreat when hurt by harsh or unmerited criticism, but if they retreat with the intention of ploughing their own furrow and sticking to it, that is all to the good. Not only do the heart and mind take over when no one is looking over an author's shoulder, the unconscious takes over, too.

And so we come to another signpost – the author's greatest friend, the unconscious mind (all too often referred to, wrongly, as the subconscious). It works for him even when the conscious one is occupied with day-to-day chores. It even works for him when sleeping. To wake up in the night, suddenly aware of a solution to a tricky situation, an elusive sentence, or to a telling title, is a common experience amongst practising authors. That is why a jotting pad and pencil at a writer's bedside are almost vital necessities. I recommend them to all beginners.

A great deal more can be done to slay the dragon of discouragement. If, for instance, you are attending writing classes but seem unable to produce what your tutor is looking for, while others in your class do so with apparent ease, don't throw it all away in despair or, even worse, decide to give up.

Tutors of writing can be of tremendous value to beginners by offering inspiration and encouragement, by detailing basic fiction structures, by recommending worthwhile reading matter, and by concentrating on grammar and composition, on syntax and style, but at that stage too many would-be writers decide that they must lack what it takes because their tutor has begun to shake his or her head rather ruefully and to mark their work negatively while, at the same time, suggesting in all kindness that perhaps they have not really been listening or concentrating. I have even heard of tutors sadly suggesting that the student should try some other art form (and writing *is* an art form, no matter how non-writers may classify it). Or perhaps the tutor himself seems genuinely disappointed, which makes the tyro feel guilty and, even worse, a failure.

It is that monster I want to help you to overcome.

The first step is to remember that teachers in *any* creative field are not oracles. However sincere their intentions and however greatly your classmates may seem to please them, remember that a tutor's selection of exemplary fiction will often be chosen according to his personal taste. He may well have excellent judgment, but it is still his individual choice. If it happens to be the student's too, well and good. In studying style and approach and every other aspect of the chosen model, an aspiring author will learn a lot but, again, must beware of slavish imitation. To model your style and approach on that of another can retard your development as an author. You must speak with your own voice.

Vaulting the hurdles

You don't have to be a high jumper to scale the initial difficulties which beset most new writers. They are by no means insurmountable unless you believe them to be. The mere fact that you *want* to write can help you to overcome the lot. In fact, this very desire means that you are half way there.

So let's examine these hurdles.

Very common is the difficulty of taking the first running jump. More often than not this is caused by fear; fear of being unable to express yourself, fear of the pristine page, fear of making a mess of it, fear of marring it with bad prose, fear of it remaining in its pristine condition after a long and fruitless session spent in staring at a blank sheet of paper which refuses to be filled.

It is a dreadful feeling, but you are not unique in experiencing it and there is a practical way of overcoming it.

It has been said that the bravest thing a writer can do is to put down the first word, but this is precisely what you *must* do and you don't have to have an idea in your head to do it. Stop searching frantically for an opening or for some arresting phrase that will usher in more at pell-mell speed; stop beating your brains for the right word because at this stage *any* word will do. One word leads to another, slowly and perhaps painfully but gathering momentum. Write anything and follow where the words lead. Tear them up if you want to, but if so *you must immediately start again.*

It is rather like the old party game of Consequences, writing down a sentence and then passing it to someone else to add another, except that in this instance the game is played solo, with the result that some sequence does form and in the process the once pristine page becomes ink-covered, proving that you *can* put your mind to it, you *can* write, you *can* compose sentences and paragraphs and chapters.

I recommend this as an exercise whenever you experience self-doubt. You will be surprised by what comes out of it, and more particularly by the way it sparks ideas, and once ideas begin to form the next page will begin to show purpose and direction.

Another difficulty (and a frightening one) can be the inability to follow up success. You have sold your first novel or short story and the publisher has asked for another, but your mind goes blank. Enter self-doubt again, then panic, then the conviction that you are a 'one-off' author, incapable of producing more. You force yourself, but produce very inferior stuff which persuades you that your conviction is justified. You have a rejected script to prove it, and when it continues to be rejected you withdraw from your writers' circle or literary group because you know that everyone is waiting to hear of your next success. Failure embarrasses and even humiliates you, so you retreat.

This psychological problem is harder to deal with than the earlier one because no amount of hammered out words come to your rescue. There is only one thing to do, stop hammering and stop asking yourself whether your one solitary success can only have been a flash in the pan. Look back on your achievement instead and acknowledge that you would never have accomplished that much if you lacked ability. Proof that you *can* write is there, staring you in the face.

So why can't you repeat it? The answer is really very simple. You are pushing yourself too hard; you are in too much of a hurry, too impatient, too anxious. You must relax and renew your acquaintanceship with reading, which you have almost certainly neglected while striving to follow up one success with another as quickly as possible.

That highly respected author and critic, Thomas Hinde, once remarked to me that 'if a writer isn't writing it's because he isn't reading.' He was right. So this is the time when instead of writing, writing, writing you must start reading, reading, reading. Not to copy, but to absorb.

Steep yourself in the works of others, but not necessarily of the genre you are specifically aiming for because the danger would, again, be that of unconscious mimicry. It is the easiest thing in the world, almost inevitable, that when you have finished reading a particular author whose writing absorbs you, you will, quite unawares, start aping their style and that style is almost sure to be wrong for you because you are a different writer, a different person with a different voice, hence the need to steep yourself in a wide and varied range of literature, absorbing the *feel* of words just as, when listening to good music, you absorb the ebb and flow of sound.

The value of reading other people's books cannot be over-stressed. You get a sort of literary feed-back, stirring your own creativity. When that happens, the need to express yourself will become insistent, but don't be in a hurry. I have read many a hopeful author's story which has been dashed off too speedily, thereby ruining it.

I know one particular person who complains that her novels are rejected because publishers and agents misjudge them. She also prides herself on the speed at which she reads, and samples of her unsold stories prove them to have been written in the same way. It often happens that a too-speedy reader will be a too-speedy writer, and that brings me to the final signpost – the way to read, and the way to extract the utmost help from it.

Reading twice over

You will find, as you develop as a writer, that you read everything with a far more critical eye than you would if you were not one. You will also listen, in the same way, to every line of dialogue in a radio or television play. This is good, this is as it should be, though I sometimes infuriate my husband by saying aloud the next line of dialogue before the actor does (this is easy with predictable dialogue; not so easy if well-written) but as far as reading is concerned I read, twice over, anything I have particularly enjoyed. In time you may well find yourself doing the same because you will no longer read as a library borrower dipping into a book merely for entertainment or relaxation.

If you fear that a lot of enjoyment will go out of reading once you cease to be uncritical, try my method – which, I am sure, is likely to be that of many another author. First read a book just as you would normally, in a relaxed and receptive frame of mind. You are sure to do this with authors whom you admire and you will also do it with an author whom you are reading for the first time and whose book, if you don't like it, you will probably put aside anyway (though as your skill develops as an author you will automatically search for the reasons for your dislike).

Now read the book again, but more slowly and with a different approach. This time you are going to find out just why you enjoy that particular author, or why you feel he or she didn't come up to scratch this time. Pay attention to the construction of the novel, the way in which problems are handled, the way in which one situation leads to another or grows out of another; pay especial attention to the time factor and how the author moves his cast from place to place or from scene to scene without interrupting the flow or the rhythm of the story, and pay equal attention to the characters, to their behaviour and their dialogue and the skilful way in which they are portrayed – because it is the characters who bring stories to life.

It may help, in your analysis, if you sketch an outline of the book or, if you prefer to merely summarize, jot down questions and answers. Why did you enjoy it so much? Was it due to the action or to the characterization, to the setting or to the subtlety of atmosphere, to the pace and style? Then examine those things more closely, studying the opening and closing of chapters and the way in which the curtain rose and fell as scene followed scene before its final descent.

If you fear that this analytical approach will spoil the novel for you, or that it will distance you from the book or stale the memory of it, you are in for a surprise. You will feel closer to it than before, as if in some way you have taken part in its creation. I have even been left with an almost proprietory feeling toward the characters, like a parent toward a family.

And how much you will have learned during this critical process! So much that you cannot wait to take up your pen and face that stack of blank paper.

So now – let's do just that.

2
Creating a Story

Getting started

Popular fiction has many faces and many names: Crime, Thrillers, Mystery, Romance, Suspense, Romantic Suspense, Espionage, Westerns, Gothic, Historical, Science Fiction, Fantasy, Humour, Occult, Horror. The categories are seemingly endless, but all have the same basic requirements; good characterization, a good plot, and the author's genuine enthusiasm for whatever genre he or she is aiming for.

Any story written tongue-in-cheek will be spotted at once by experienced editors and publishers, and rejected – and will deserve to be. Every work of fiction or non-fiction must be written because the author *wants* to write it, because he cannot rest until he does, because even if it is rejected and continues to be, that rejection will become a challenge and a challenge stimulates a mind which is intent on achieving a particular goal.

So after the initial and often bitter disappointment, the author with a passionate urge to write will push a rejected typescript out of sight and begin again. The chances are that he will have already started something else without waiting for a verdict on the first, and when he returns to the rejected one after completing the second he will find that after such a lapse of time the whole thing will be seen in better perspective and with a keener and more critical eye.

However strong the temptation, I urge every aspiring author never to make the mistake of discarding a rejected manuscript in a mood of self-disgust or even greater self-doubt, nor of immediately submitting it to another publisher without first re-reading it in an attempt to assess whether its rejection was justified, and for what reason. The chances that unsuspected flaws will now leap from the page are high, especially if the script is put away for a prolonged period.

There is no need for one rejection, or even more, to make you abandon hope. Stories of books being published after a chain of rejections are numerous. A notable one is that of James Hilton's *Goodbye Mr Chips*, turned down by fourteen book publishers until an American magazine published it as a complete 'one shot' (a compact supplement at the end of the issue) because of its brevity. It proved so popular that book publishers competed for the right to publish this short and delightful story. What happened after that is well known.

In many cases, however, books published after a chain of rejections are likely to have been rewritten and reshaped where necessary, often at the suggestion of a publisher's editor but sometimes after the author has had the good sense to accept the *challenge* of rejection, and to learn from it.

Another important thing to realise is that there is nothing personal about a rejection. 'Publishers don't seem to *like* me!' wailed one unsuccessful author I know. She remained unconvinced despite my pointing out that no publisher or editor could have any personal prejudice against someone they did not know, that a manuscript could be rejected for one of many reasons – because others of a similar genre happened to be in the stockpile (a reason unlikely to apply to specific category lists in which a publisher may specialize, such as crime), or that, for the moment, they were not publishing any more novels for economic reasons, or it was the type of book they never published anyway, as the author could have discovered by studying library shelves or buying a copy of *Writers' & Artists' Yearbook* or *The Writer's Handbook* and turning to publishers' listings. There can be a dozen reasons for rejection, and none of them personal.

Once an author begins to believe that rejection is due to personal prejudice, a red light should flash. If he allows such an idea to persist he may be heading for the psychiatrist's couch!

Three vital ingredients

In addition to enthusiasm for his story, an author needs the two other essentials referred to earlier – good characterization and a good plot. These three requirements are predominant in all types of popular fiction because the aim is the same in all categories – to tell a story with a beginning, a middle, and an end.

The variations (the individual demands of background, time, place, theme and genre) will all develop from there. Remember that the construction of a romantic novel or a crime novel or any other work of fiction differs from other categories only within its particular parameters.

But *how* to start? How to create that plot and those believable characters?

Which comes first – plotting or characterization?

There is a common belief that the first step in writing fiction is to draw up a plot, and the second is simply to slot in some characters. Easy! you think. So you draw one up and devise situation after situation and development after development and you're off and away.

But are you? Think again. Do you really know the people whom you expect to fit so easily into your preconceived plan? How do they think, feel, react? Where do they come from? How have they been brought up? What influences have moulded their characters? Are they really the type of people to willingly dance like puppets to your tune? Wouldn't they prefer to dance to one of their own? And wouldn't they, being human, do precisely that, tangling the threads of your plot and leaving you stranded or at least hopelessly muddled?

To me, slotting characters into a preconceived plan would be like pinning cardboard figures on a map, and there is certainly a danger that a story so contrived will be unconvincing.

I am sure Humbert Wolfe was speaking from experience when he said that in good fiction one couldn't just rig up a plot and push the characters in afterwards; that the plot, the story, could only arise from the characters themselves. Somerset Maugham said the same thing and historian Edward Gibbon endorsed it when saying that history is little more than a register of the crimes, follies and misfortunes of mankind. Pick up any newspaper and you will see how right all of them were.

It is *people* who create plots; *people* who hold hostages to ransom, dethrone kings, kidnap children, intrigue politically, commit murder and rape and robbery; hold wives, husbands, parents, children and lovers in emotional bondage – or conversely (and omitted from Gibbon's list) achieve great things, commit acts of heroism and many romantic and unselfish deeds. Of such stuff and from such people are stories made.

Look back on your own life, how much of it have you been personally responsible for? How many decisions have you made and stuck to because you felt they were right, irrespective of other people's opinions? How many things have you deliberately changed, or deliberately decided to do, and what were the results? And how often have you said 'If only I had done this . . . or that . . .' and then tried to visualise the outcome either way, making comparisons with your actual choice?

It is an undeniable fact that most people, intentionally or unintentially, are responsible for many events in their lives. Not every twist and turn can be attributed solely to fate. We make choices, sometimes wisely and sometimes foolishly, but we make them all the same. Within our limitations and within the circumstances into which we were born we are responsible for a large part of our destinies, and as a result many of us overcome our limitations and our circumstances. So, too, do fictional characters. If you live with them, letting them simmer in your mind until you really *know* them, you will understand them, empathise with them, and give them their heads. You will then find that the claim of many authors that 'their characters take over' is not far from the truth.

The basic story idea will be yours, but the development and action come from the characters. That action must always be in keeping with their natures, since it is from their natures that it springs. So even when your hands are in control you must allow your characters to share the reins, otherwise they will pull against you and your story will run into difficulties. You must continuously ask yourself such questions as: 'Would he *do* such a thing?' 'Would *she* be happy and at ease in such a situation?' '*Would* such a couple behave that way?' 'Would such behaviour be *natural* in such a man. . . .?'

So I give you one golden rule – get your characters first.

You don't agree? Then let's find out.

The growth of a story

In her book, *Pen to Paper*, the late Pamela Frankau related how, when teaching English at a Post-Hostilities School of Army Education, she suggested one day that the class should write a short story. Asking where they would begin and what they would look for first, she received the united answer of 'Plot!' Characters, they declared, could then follow, so it was agreed that she should set the plot and they would provide the characters.

The plot concerned a murderer who invited his two victims to dinner. His chosen method of killing was to screw down the dining room ceiling on top of them, crushing them to death, but at the last minute the victims were to be saved by the floor collapsing and dropping them a short distance into a cellar, out of harm's way.

The students accepted the plot unanimously and then set to work to produce the main character – the murderer. They gave the matter a great deal of thought and as they created him she listed the details on the blackboard. They decided on a civil servant and because of that, to their way of thinking, he had to be mousey and middle aged – and of course he had a mousey little middle aged wife. He did his job adequately, was never late for the office, caught the same commuter trains morning and evening, drove neither a car nor a motor-bike. He liked gardening, took his seaside holiday at the same place every year, was practically teetotal, a bad sailor, and paid his bills regularly. He was not much of a reader, certainly not of novels or poetry. A nice enough guy, in his way. Rather shy, with an inability to make close friends but always pleasant and well-mannered.

On the blackboard he was a complete and believable character. Then came the task of fitting him into the plot. She summed him up. A nice, timid, unadventurous chap; fond of routine and peace; no particular discontent; no hobbies except his garden; no mechanical knowledge, no special skills. The temperature began to drop, so she pressed on. Would he, not even a car driver or the owner of a motor bike, be of a sufficiently mechanical turn of mind to devise a screw-down ceiling in order to commit this murder? And who were the enemies of this mild, dutiful, garden-loving man? Where were his motives?

At a stroke, the plot collapsed – and we are back to my golden rule. Get your characters first, and they will lead you to your plot . . . which leads *us* straight into exercises for character and plot building.

Variations on a theme

Exercise number one. Let's take a man with similar characteristics – we'll make him a retired schoolmaster and call him Horace – and consider how one of his nature *would* commit murder, and whom he would want to kill.

Since he has no enemies, and is a quiet, reserved man without friends, wouldn't his life be bound up in his wife? And haven't the mildest of men been driven to murder throughout the course of history? One can see this meek, dutiful, routine-minded man simmering slowly to boiling point over a long period of time, bottling up resentment against his wife for imprisoning him in monotony, feeling cheated by her for not remaining the desirable woman he had once found her and quite unaware that *he* has ceased to be desirable to *her*. . . .

In such a man, resentments could also be fanned by the success of working colleagues who have outstripped him, successively cheating him out of the headmastership he has always coveted and who apparently have all that he would regard as the trappings of success – a better house, a bigger garden, holidays abroad instead of annually at Skegness tied to his wife's skirts – but the murder poor Horace would commit would be too unimaginative to demand any James Bond stunts; more likely it would be a quiet, slow kind of murder, full of the surprising cunning that quiet, slow people can sometimes reveal.

And it could be the obvious one which any writer, given such a character, might make the first choice. Since the man is a keen gardener he could have access to weed killer, the purchase of which is legal and would therefore arouse neither comment nor curiousity, especially at the local garden centre where he is known as a regular customer. He would also know, as all gardeners do, that certain weedkillers contain arsenic and, being intelligent enough to hold down his job adequately, he would be sufficiently intelligent to check on the effects of arsenic on the human body, using the reference room at his local library because he would not be so unwise as to buy books on poisons and keep them on his bookshelves or hidden somewhere in the house.

He would therefore be aware that arsenic is odourless and virtually tasteless, especially if administered in small doses over a period of time – in, say, the nice cup of tea he takes to his wife first thing every morning (the dear, devoted husband that he is). 'Four lumps as usual, Ethel dear. That sweet tooth of yours'll be the death of you yet!' I can see this quiet, gentle man enjoying that joke and his wife not getting it at all.

And he would not make a special visit to the library to do his checking. Being a man of routine, he would do it when returning books for himself and his wife, as he has done every week throughout their married life, and if he came back a little later than usual one evening he could easily make the excuse that he had had difficulty, this time, in finding the nice romantic novel she was wanting by her favourite Mills & Boon author – and no excuse might even be necessary because the dull, mousey little woman has probably fallen asleep in front of the goggle-box and not even missed him.

But since poison is known to be mainly a woman's instrument, another murder method could be thought up for such a man. He could go berserk and kill his wife with an axe or carving knife, exploding after years of pent-up and slowly corroding hatred – this would be dramatic, but not, I think, as suspenseful as a cunning, quietly thought out murder because a crime of such violence could not be covered up, or appear to be death by natural causes. And it would surely focus suspicion on him, however hard he tried to make out that a killer had broken in, whereas a record of stomach disorders and bouts of sickness over a period of time could establish a pattern of ill health and scarcely arouse comment since he had unfailingly called the doctor every time his wife had 'one of her billious attacks'.

So how will he go about it and will-he-won't-he get away with it? How will the truth be discovered and bring him to justice? That is the exercise you must now go to work on, bearing in mind that if you want your story to be convincing rather than contrived all his actions and reactions must stem from his basic nature.

Finding alternatives

The foregoing random thoughts restrict the tale to the crime category, but this retired schoolmaster and his wife offer other possibilities, bringing us to exercise number two, which takes them into another genre.

Let's see them as a typical Darby and Joan, celebrating their Golden or Diamond Wedding, a situation which could switch them into the sphere of romance, which is by no means confined to boy-meets-girl. We have now changed routes and landed in the world of sentiment, the old couple's love story ready to be relived with all its problems and its passions, its triumphs and disasters. This means that the personality and character of the wife must be developed as vividly as the husband's since she will have as great a part to play. It also means that the story can be written from either viewpoint.

Alternatively, still in the world of sentiment but not writing in retrospect, we can plunge into the family celebration with the children and grandchildren who have come from far and near. But this, however, merely sets the scene. What of the plot? What of developments? In this category of fiction the theme must be wholly emotional and, again, this will be dictated by the characters themselves, by the depth of family affection, by filial devotion or lack of it, by jealousies and loves, even by hopes and dreams.

In yet another step we can move into the field of straight magazine fiction, aiming for a market which publishes stories of social significance or psychological interest. We can write it from the angle of the wife who, after fifty years of silent and dutiful devotion, is goaded into tearing the blinkers from her husband's eyes by revealing long-suppressed feelings; resentment, frustration, regret because she remained loyal to him and to their growing family and resisted the temptation to run away with another man, and now it is too late. Do her smouldering thoughts ignite to the point where she strikes back? If so, how? And what is the outcome?

Such a situation has boundless possibilities. It could be psychologically chilling or even, perhaps, funny if all she could do to celebrate the occasion was to hit him over the head with a flower pot or, for a sinister twist, something much heavier. Promptly, your story-telling mind is asking, 'And what happened then?', 'How would such a woman then behave?'

Or how about writing it from their family's viewpoint? Let's imagine the kind of children and grandchildren this elderly couple would have and the way in which they themselves, in contrast, had been brought up, and immediately we have double generation gaps and triple social standards. A moving and even disturbing picture of that family re-union could then be built up, with the interplay of family misunder-standings, the inability of different generations to see eye to eye or to enjoy the same things, and the gradual surfacing of emotional under-currents.

Such a story could be tragi-comic or sad, or given a happy ending with the intolerance of the young slowly evaporating as they realise that their grandparents are more understanding and more likeable than they expected and, after coming to the party unwillingly, they ask how soon they may come again.

Take any of these situations, and develop them for yourself. That is exercise number two.

For exercise number three let's take Horace on his own and move him into yet another genre. This time we will make him an eccentric widower, living alone in a terraced London house, his only visitor being a cleaner-lady who 'does for him' daily and *she* knows better than to set foot in that attic where he spends all day and every day. Doing what? Nobody knows or cares until strange things begin to happen in this very respectable street; strange sounds emanate through that attic window, and then strange shapes are seen, and the cleaner-lady suddenly refuses to come back (or maybe she disappears?), then, one by one, fantastic creatures emerge and take over the street . . . and we're off into the science fiction category with Horace, the sci-fi fanatic, appalled (or excited) by the outcome of his secret experiments. (And of course, for the horror genre, you could make the creatures truly horrific, with horrific events and horrific results. Stephen King and Dean Koontz, watch out!)

For further variations on character and theme, we can take Horace into yet more categories; mystery, gothic, or even quirky humour with some scheming lady taking advantage of his loneliness to lead him to the altar, then giving the tale an ironic twist by making him guess what she is after and thwarting her by settling his money on his scattered children in order to avoid death duties, reserving only sufficient to maintain himself and his home and the services of his ready-made, unpaid, and frustrated housekeeper.

Or, rather more romantically, we could imagine him as a Mr Chips type of character; endearing, lovable, possibly meeting again his first youthful love, now widowed.

And what about the realms of history? Decide on a famous or infamous character whose story fascinates you. For example, a king such as Richard III, portrayed as a monster by Shakespeare and more sympathetically by Josephine Tey in *Daughter of Time*; a man championed today by a vociferous society of supporters, but whose name remains associated with the murder of the princes in the Tower. Get a postcard or print of his famous portrait from the National Gallery and see what you detect in that patient, gentle, rather sad face. You may not see any of those qualities in it, but only quiet cunning, representing the first aspect we attributed to our retired schoolmaster. Ponder on it, and you may be off into the historical genre with yet another story about that apparently notorious king.

The foregoing demonstrates how, from one character alone, a chain of ideas can spring. The permutations are endless so, for exercise number four, see how many more you can come up with about a man with Horace's characteristics, but bear in mind that each and every twist and every new variation of plot must not only involve him but emanate from him, aided and abetted by supporting characters. As the central figure, he must be the pivot of the story. The main character is always at the centre of conflict, his problem the issue which runs through the tale and holds it together by giving it motivation.

The word 'conflict' does not necessarily mean the physical kind. It can be purely emotional. Conflicting ambitions, conflicting aims, conflicting loves, conflicting views; whatever the type of conflict it must be *there*, centre stage.

It is also important to remember that supporting characters must never hog the limelight, so if you find that another character is threatening to take command, think again. You may have someone stronger who will lead you to a stronger plot, with Horace now relegated to a supporting role.

Remember, too, that each and every character must have an essential part to play. If they don't contribute to the story's development, even in the smallest way, cut them out; they will clutter the scene and interrupt the action. Unnecessary characters are dead wood that no story can afford to carry.

But, staying with our imaginary Horace, remember too that in whatever category you wish to slot him, he won't fit into it unless his character changes fundamentally every time, and it won't do that unless you see him and know him thoroughly, so in whatever guise you dress him, leave him to grow in your mind. Don't hurry him. Don't rush anything. A story, like a plant, can grow only at its own pace and with the right nurturing.

And now, for exercise number five, replace this man with someone created wholly by yourself. This is important, not only to stretch your imagination but to help you to avoid the temptation, consciously or unconsciously, of stealing characters created by other writers. Yes, I know Jean Rhys did it in *Wide Sargasso Sea*, her brilliant and wholly imaginative story about Mr Rochester's mad wife in *Jane Eyre*, but in no way is her novel a pastiche of Charlotte Brontë, nor does it encroach on the Brontë book in the slightest degree. *Wide Sargasso Sea* is a totally independent story about a character who, to Charlotte Brontë, was no more than a lunatic locked up in an attic and branded, in the author's imagination, by her Creole blood, but this tragic character haunted Jean Rhys for years because it awakened her own memories of life in the West Indies as the daughter of a Creole mother who was herself one of the tragic Creole heiresses of the nineteenth century. Only if you can create something equally individual do you need no warnings from me.

So now pick up pen and pad again and start inventing a character uniquely your own, then try it out in various situations designed for various genre, as we did with Horace. When you find that the character fits into one more naturally than into another, you will have discovered the category you need to aim for.

3
Getting Ideas

Sources

You can find ideas anywhere and everywhere. In newspapers and magazines; in shops and trains; from people chattering in buses; from your own problems or those of friends; from trying to imagine, as I suggested earlier, what would have happened had you made a different choice at a certain time in your life; from political crises; from politicians' slanging matches; from a line of dialogue in film or play; from backgrounds; from ancient houses; from people and places and even from things.

For instance, what does a piece of shattered china suggest to you? A clumsy visitor, a burglary, a fraught wife venting her frustration, a child trying to please its mother by doing the washing up, a shopper accidentally dislodging a counter display and being pounced on by the manager?

The world is full of ideas, if you look for them. You can even turn up a ready-made plot in Georges Polti's *The Thirty-Six Dramatic Situations*, which contains, in embryo, almost every book or play ever written, but keeping your eyes and ears open and giving your imagination free rein can serve you better. Do this on your way to or from work, when lunching in snack bars, queueing for buses or sitting in traffic jams. Study your fellow travellers; focus your mind on one in particular and try to imagine his or her background, occupation, likes and dislikes. What sort of a house or flat do they live in, and in what sort of neighbourhood and street? Do they live alone or with boyfriend or girlfriend? Are they married? Have they children? Study their facial expression; is it gentle, pugnacious, wistful, petulant, kindly, humorous, peevish or good-natured? What are they thinking about as they sit staring idly into space?

Your answers may well be very wide of the truth, but gradually you will have your own picture of them and can start weaving your story. Imagine someone waiting for them when they reach their destination. Will they rush to meet each other or merely exchange a peck on the cheek? If only the latter, why? Is it a kiss of indifference from a married partner who has come only from a sense of duty, or is it a kiss of shyness because they don't know each other intimately yet? So what lies ahead? Give your imagination free rein; let it come up with whatever notion it fancies. By the time you reach your own destination it will be going full blast.

Ideas can also come from sayings or from song titles, from poetry remembered from childhood, from proverbs and quotations, and from chance remarks. My novel, *The Mating Dance*, sprang from a comment of David Attenborough's during one of his TV documentaries, and another made to me many years earlier by an actor, Nigel Patrick. Nigel's parents had been professional actors and I had never forgotten him telling me, as we foot-slogged between theatrical agencies around Shaftesbury Avenue and the Charing Cross Road one long ago morning during my unsuccessful theatrical days, that he had actually been born in a dressing room. His mother had continued to perform right up to the time of his birth (luckily it was a period piece and required flowing robes) and when he decided to arrive in a hurry her theatrical skip had been used as a cradle.

(At this point I feel I should stress that when needing to demonstrate how to handle a specific writing problem, I will either make up a simple illustration or quote from my own published work. I can then speak from personal experience and explain the intention behind it with greater authority. Exceptions will occur when I wish to pay tribute to a particular writer's ingenuity or skill.)

So how were the remarks of David Attenborough and Nigel Patrick linked, and how did they spark a novel set in the Victorian theatre-world?

'This is their mating dance,' said David Attenborough as two exotic birds weaved and pranced, and 'What a title for a book!' I said to my husband. I let the title simmer until, over a period of months, the background suggested itself. The word 'dance' indicated a frequent change of partner, and frequent change suggested promiscuity, and *that* suggested a world where it was commonplace. Promiscuity now being openly indulged, another period was essential. I chose the Victorian, in which immorality was taboo in respectable circles, but not in the theatrical world. Then I recalled Nigel Patrick's story and there I was, in a theatrical dressing room.

The opening setting was ready to hand, but not the characters. All I could see was the newborn child lying in a battered theatrical skip; no one else, not even the mother. I knew she was an actress, but no more than that because she stubbornly refused to come to life. I therefore came to a dead halt. Finally I abandoned the idea of a child being born, but retained the setting. Even then, and despite laborious mental searching, I could people that dressing room with nothing more than a glamorous leading lady, glitter, romance, gushing admirers, adoring Stagedoor Johnnies, champagne, the popping of corks, ogling and laughter and artificiality.

But that wasn't what I wanted. It was trite. The opening had to be more down to earth, more realistic, and more dramatic. Finally despairing I abandoned it, but the setting refused to let me go. So did the newborn child. For weeks my mind kept advancing and retreating, haunting the place, seeing nothing but a picture of an actress giving birth after the curtain had fallen, an actress without face or form. Something was wrong.

Questions began to plague me. How soon would she be acting again and who would take her place in the meantime? If she had continued to perform right up to the moment of her child's birth, plainly she had no understudy, so that character was ruled out. I had reached a dead end when the first really constructive answer hit me. *It was not the leading lady who gave birth, but another woman, one who would always be in the dressing room with her – her dresser.*

Promptly, I was asking how the leading lady would react to such an inconvenient event and *then* things began to fall into place, and so did the necessary characters for my opening scene. Beyond that, I could visualise nothing. I made no outline. I put pen to paper and sought the first line, letting it lead me where it willed. My first paragraph flowed:

> I was literally born to the smell of greasepaint, inhaling it with my first breath in the dressing room of the great Bernadette Boswell during a matinee on June 16, 1880, an indiscretion for which she never wholly forgave my mother. It was not the privilege of dressers to give birth in star dressing rooms, leaving the leading lady unbuttoned all the way down the back and the call-boy shouting 'Beginners, please!' outside the door.

Following a mere thread I had established the place, the period, the time of day, the characters who were to start the story and relevant facts about each. I had written what is known as a narrative hook (on which I will enlarge in Chapter 8), an opening paragraph designed to lead, as all opening paragraphs should, to the question of what happened next.

I hadn't a clue. I was an onlooker, watching the characters, and because they had been growing in my mind I knew that the leading lady was an overbearing woman who would consider such an event not only inconvenient but outrageous. I knew she would therefore go rushing to the wings, shouting for help, not for her dresser, but for herself, her only thought being that someone had to button her up, her selfishness clearly indicating her inability to forgive (a characteristic which would plainly increase as the novel grew, and so influence developments). So another character had to enter, preferably without knocking for admission. The identity of that person was obvious.

Married couples often share dressing rooms, or have communicating ones, so the entry of the great Bernadette's husband was inevitable. In he came, hurrying to see what was wrong and finding the poor dresser in a mighty predicament. And of course one question about the dresser hit me. Why was she working so near her time? Surely the average husband, however poor, wouldn't let her? Answer: she had no husband, so needed the money, and the child's illegitimacy became important to the story.

This is how plots spring from characters. Their actions and reactions spark situations and their problems create others.

But that is just one example. Let's take another, not from a title or a quotation this time, but from a remark I actually overheard in a New York restaurant on my first visit very many years ago. Two women were sitting at the next table, close enough for their conversation to be unavoidably overheard. I have never forgotten it.

'And how's Mary-Lou?' asked one.

'Oh, she's fine,' said the other. 'She's just made her first marriage.'

Perhaps it was naïve of me to find the remark astonishing. In those days America had the highest divorce rate in the world, so the lack of reaction from the woman's companion, other than mild interest, should not have surprised me either.

'That so?' said she. 'A good one?'

'Good enough, I guess.'

Good enough to go on with? Good enough until she finds another? Good enough until she does better for herself? Was that what the woman actually meant?

This immediately sparked the idea for a short story about an ambitious mother who disapproved of her daughter's marriage to a man considered (by ambitious Mama) to be reasonably acceptable socially but rather less so financially; a good enough stop-gap, but no more. By the time I returned to England the story was alive in my head; the story of a scheming mother with an ugly-duckling daughter married off to a passable man while Mama remained hopeful that someone more acceptable would turn up to be husband number two.

With maturity, the daughter blossomed and Mama's hopes soared. With calculated cunning the woman cast her net, entertaining on a scale she could not afford, manipulating introductions to a higher social scale and focusing on successful men – in particular, on a thrice-divorced and wealthy financier who would make a highly acceptable son-in-law. She also expended time and energy in determinedly breaking up her daughter's marriage.

All went according to plan. The desired divorce went through and to her mother's satisfaction the girl willingly let the eminent man squire her around, being seen everywhere in his chauffeur-driven Rolls which he, obviously smitten, indulgently suggested she should use when shopping. Much elated, scheming Mama began to brag to all and sundry about her new son-in-law-to-be until, to her horror, the daughter eloped with a man even poorer and less socially acceptable than the first, the chauffeur, leaving dear Mama not only financially embarrassed but socially embarrassed as well.

Put baldly, the plot was slight, but it lent itself well to a 3,000-word script and the characters were alive because they were vivid to me. I quote it only as an example of how chance remarks can give birth to ideas.

What about other sources? A newspaper item, perhaps. Let's take an imaginary one from a small town journal, and see what ideas it sparks.

MISSING WOMAN RETURNS AFTER TWENTY-FIVE YEARS

Elspeth Marshall was twenty-three when she disappeared from her home in the village of Woodfield, leaving her husband, Joseph Marshall, proprietor of The White Horse, and a two-year-old daughter. Prolonged searching yielded no trace. Her disappearance coincided with a series of murders in the vicinity and the police were finally forced to conclude that she had been a victim, though her body was never found. Joseph Marshall eventually remarried, but was recently killed in a car crash. Elspeth Marshall has refused to be interviewed.

Your imagination can really run riot here. Where had she been for the last twenty-five years? Why had she gone? What drove a young mother to leave her husband and child? How had she been living since then, and with whom? The newspaper gives no details other than the bare facts of her disappearance, so you can weave any imaginary pictures that appeal to you.

Start yet again by asking yourself questions. Has she returned because she has heard of her husband's death and thinks she can claim the profitable village pub? After all, he has married bigamously so his current wife can surely have no legal claim to it. Or has she returned because her daughter is now grown up and she hopes to make her understand her mother's actions and to be reunited with her? And, if so, how will the daughter react? She will now be twenty-seven and possibly married; she may well have left the village and even if she has not, she probably has no recollection of her mother. All she knows is that she was abandoned by her at the age of two. Hardly someone to put out the welcome mat for.

Having answered these questions, and any others your imagination conjures up, decide on the angle from which you intend to start. How about that of the woman who is now, legally or otherwise, the 'official' Mrs Marshall? Is she tough or timid? Would she be determined not to be ousted from this profitable and comfortable inn which is not only her source of income but her home? Does she believe that possession *is* nine points of the law? Has Joseph Marshall left a will, or not? Does a legal wrangle ensue? And on whose side would the daughter be? Is the relationship between stepmother and stepdaughter strong, or shaky? A battle between three members of the same sex could certainly develop from this angle.

Or go off on a totally different tack. The Elspeth Marshall who returns is rich and successful, proprietor of a prominent chain of boutiques selling way-out teenage gear. She was penniless when she disappeared, so from where did she get the money to launch such a business? Her surname is unchanged and there appears to be no man in her life. So how did her successful career get started and what brings her back to a quiet country village where the inhabitants are mainly middle-aged or elderly, its only attraction being the popularity of The White Horse for weekenders? Could it be the proximity of a rapidly growing town only a few miles distant? Does she feel that, now her husband is really out of the way, she can open a branch there, buy a house in her native village, settle down and, believing that money can buy anything, expect to be accepted by the local inhabitants, many of whom may have lived there all their lives? And how do the inhabitants react to her? How long is their memory?

With thought, you can come up with a variety of plots from this imaginary newspaper item. My personal choice would be to tell the story through the eyes of the daughter who, quietly and determinedly, probes for the truth about her mother's past and keeps silent about it until such time that she chooses. This approach could lead to bitterness or to sympathetic understanding, but either way it would yield conflict; that essential quality in all storytelling. Conflict would come from the daughter if she could not forgive her mother, and the daughter would also experience strong emotional conflict if, *in* forgiving her, she felt disloyal to her father. And there would be inevitable conflict between the first wife and the second.

Scenes of emotional conflict present great scope because emotion comes from the heart. All writing should come from the heart if it is to attract and hold the reader's attention.

You will have noticed that the news item I made up was short and of no world-wide or national interest. When scouring press columns for ideas, always look for the buried paragraph, the seemingly unimportant, even the trivial. Never latch on to the latest sensation, or the biggest scandal, or any highly topical theme. If you do, you will almost certainly share the fate of dozens of other writers whose typescripts will be boomeranging back from editorial offices which have been inundated with stories based on the same sensation, a sensation being flogged to death by the media and with which the public is rapidly becoming bored.

'But,' you argue, 'lots of famous criminal cases and notorious scandals have been turned into novels!' True. Judith Rosner's *Looking for Mr Goodbar* is an example. Based on a tragic real life murder case in America, the book succeeded because it far excelled others based on the same tragedy (some of which were published, but eclipsed), but the advice I give throughout this book is mainly for the inexperienced writer and unless you happen to be a natural genius (in which case you need no help from me) you would be wise to avoid competition with the many other writers who seize on the latest sensations.

The best use for ideas gleaned from press sources is for exercising the imagination, for getting the mental wheels turning, for releasing words onto paper, after which the real you will emerge, urging you to write to your own ideas.

Other sources

Some of the most creative ideas come from situations or characters which suddenly present themselves visually. To illustrate this I must again quote from personal experience.

My novel, *Dragonmede*, emerged from a picture which sprang to mind about two years before I started writing the book. As always with things springing from the unconscious, I have no idea where it came from, but I had a vivid mental picture of an Edwardian lady wearing a blue velvet costume trimmed with sable, and a splendid hat covered in matching blue. She carried a sable muff. Later, a child thrust herself into the picture, holding the woman's hand and skipping along happily. The woman was smiling down at her, indifferent to the fact that her own elegant skirts were sweeping the ground. That told me that the child meant more to her than her fine clothes.

Mother and child lingered with me for months. The woman had long, tapering fingers which I could imagine hovering over a silver tea-stand and delicate porcelain. Later, that was replaced with a more vivid picture of the same hands dexterously dealing a pack of cards. It was this picture that finally took hold of me, and so did a sudden question: could this fashionable lady run an exclusive card-playing salon, even a notorious one from which she would make a point of excluding her daughter as she grew up? Why not? I knew instinctively that she was warm hearted, immoral by conventional standards, protective of, and ambitious for, her daughter.

After considering the best angle from which to write, I discarded several openings and left it to the daughter, when grown up, to tell their story.

And so I began, again with no outline and only the mother and daughter in mind. Instinctively, I let the daughter's voice speak the opening lines:

> By most standards my upbringing was scandalous, though it was a long time before the fact was brought home to me. As a child I accepted, without question, the bohemian, rather shameful but happy life I lived with my mother until I was old enough to realise that it was, to say the least, unconventional, and even then I continued to accept it because whatever her mode of living, her lack of morals, and her feckless attitude to money, my mother had the rare ability to make life rich and full and warm. She lived generously and she loved generously, and more than all she loved me.

Once a picture is vivid in your mind, it will seize you, hold you, and carry you forward. The more you write, the more visually you will see everything.

Such pictures can also linger with you from scenes actually witnessed. I remember seeing a laden young soldier on Waterloo Station. He was obviously home on leave and waiting for someone. His expression was tense, his restless pacing betrayed his feelings and his fears: she wasn't coming, she had stood him up or, worse, she had met with an accident. Only someone very much in love could display such anxiety. And then a girl came running, breathless, eager: his expression changed from anxiety to joy, wordlessly they met, wordlessly they clung. I remember them to this day because a whole story of young love was there, of hope, of joy after separation. A romantic ending, or a romantic beginning? I never knew and I never made up a story about them. So why, as yet another exercise, don't you?

Witnessing a situation, and developing it, can be rewarding and since it is people who create situations they will always provide a springboard for action. Imagine seeing a woman jumping into a tube-train as the doors are closing, her trapped skirt leaving her outside and dragging her with it. Such a situation, as the train heads for the tunnel, presents mind-boggling possibilities. This is where you must tackle it with the old and tried method of question and answer.

How is she saved? By her skirt ripping at the crucial moment so that she falls onto the platform? But what if it is winter and the cloth is tough? She will be saved even more convincingly then because she will also be wearing a coat and the combined thickness of materials will prevent the doors from closing completely, signalling to the driver that something is wrong. So bang goes the germ of a plot, but the situation still holds possibilities.

Time and place have been established, but not why she steps so tardily onto the train. First you must know the type of person she is, because this will tell you why she is late. It will also give the story motivation. Is she absent-minded and, if so, why? Is she merely a day-dreamer? Perhaps she is lazy, with a tendency to oversleep or dawdle when getting ready for work. Is she emotional, her mind occupied with a lovers' quarrel? Is she a worrier who broods over problems, say a difficult mother or a fretful child (immediate introduction of other characters), or is she merely suffering from a hangover after a late party which she now regrets? So what kind of woman is she to go to the kind of parties one regrets? Who took her there and why was she willing to go? Is she weak and easily influenced?

Over to you again. I made her up so, like Elspeth Marshall in the imaginary news paragraph, I give her to you. Bring her to life; bring both to life, and their stories with them.

Places and backgrounds

These can be potent sources for ideas. To me, the very atmosphere of Glencoe conjures up the massacre of the MacDonalds, and from this sprang an earlier novel, *Glenrannoch*. In the same way, houses of all kinds can speak volumes. Empty houses, ancient houses, occupied houses; country houses and town houses; isolated cottages and ruined castles. Questions are promptly launched in my mind and I am instantly wondering who lived in such and such a place, who built it, how many people occupied it, when and for how long and, in the case of deserted buildings, why they were abandoned. *What happened there?*

Try it, and you will be surprised by what comes to mind. And in using this method, by no means will you be alone. I recall seeing crime writer P D James in a TV series featuring prominent authors. She was walking on Brownsea Island, asking herself who had built the house there, who had inhabited it, and what made them leave. Into her mind, she said, crept shadowy people and there she planned to let them remain, to take their own shape and form until eventually she knew how they looked, behaved, reacted; the things they were likely to do or not do. From them the plot would develop.

The sources for ideas that I have mentioned are but a few. You will discover more for yourself the more you write, for the more you write the more your ideas will flow.

Exercising the imagination

This chapter has been demonstrating not only how to get ideas, but how to develop them with judicious use of the imagination. There are other ways in which you can exercise this most valuable tool, without which the most brilliant plot can remain a mere skeleton. How you clothe its bones depends entirely on you. No two writers would do it the same way.

This was once put to the test by an editor named Fothergill, who hit on the idea of circulating a basic plot amongst a number of authors to develop into a short story. The results were so different that, to prove his point, he published them in an anthology. Each author had clothed the skeleton according to his own imagination, but the interesting thing is that they were all badly reviewed. 'Dull' was the general verdict, proving that a plot can be useless if it is not first inspired by a character or characters.

But the most vivid imagination can sometimes need exercising. Here are one or two ways in which to prod it.

(1) Set yourself a problem; make it as difficult as possible. Then set yourself a time limit in which to solve it; not too short and not too long. Too short would mean pressure and pressure can cause panic and panic can make the imagination dry up. Too long can lead to a feeling that you have all the time in the world, and so to laziness, and so to indifference. I suggest you give yourself two weeks in which to come to grips with it. Carry the problem in your mind wherever you go and let your imagination take over.

(2) Take a rejected story out of its hiding place and look for its weakest character. Almost unfailingly there will be one that is less effective than the rest. See how you can strengthen it. See how it affects the plot and whether, by changing the *motivation* of that character, the story can be improved. You will find yourself re-thinking the whole thing and, by changing the influence of that character, you will almost certainly produce a much better story.

(3) Timing. If you are in the middle of a story and it drags, try changing its pace. Start at an earlier point, at an incident which you have mentioned in passing. You may have missed an opportunity for action, so go back and *start* there. If there is no such incident, create one. Either way, your imagination will get a tremendous spur.

If it doesn't work, then look ahead. Perhaps you started the story too far back, so take a leap forward instead. This may provide a surprising impetus and will almost certainly spark new ideas.

Telling the tale

When I am asked how I write a novel, a question which always seems to demand some magic formula in answer, I can only say, truthfully, that I tell myself the story as I go along but, before I begin to write, certain characters and certain scenes have been simmering in my head, sometimes for a long time, sometimes briefly. This always involves the characters. Even snatches of their dialogue have come to me now and then, very often forgotten but occasionally dredged up in their entirety. If you experience the same thing but doubt your memory, jot the dialogue down without delay, also important bits of characterisation which will help you, when you start writing, to see your characters as vividly as when they first crept into your mind.

Because I see everything visually, writing a novel is, to me, rather like occupying a seat in the stalls and watching the whole thing unfold before me. That is what makes a story come alive for me, though of course it is really the characters who do that. It is when I am actually writing that I see them in action, hear them talking and, with a novelist's privilege, am allowed to know what they are thinking and feeling.

Which brings me to the vital subject of characterization.

4
Characterization

Bringing your characters to life

Many professional storytellers are hard pressed to answer a question frequently asked by aspiring authors, 'How do you make your characters convincing?' The longer many novelists have been published, the more inarticulate they seem to be on the subject, answering vaguely that they 'just come alive somehow', or that 'somehow they just grow'.

The reason is that, with experience, the majority of authors have ceased to be unduly anxious about this particular aspect. They are familiar with the way in which characters take hold and know that if they devote sufficient thought to them they will develop and change as the story develops and changes (as we ourselves develop and change in the progression of our lives). Nor are they surprised when a character, who initially promised to be important, proves to be otherwise and must therefore be discarded.

Some books on the writing of fiction include several pages devoted to the subject of characterization, all of which sound very knowledgeable but which yield nothing constructive or even inspiring. Such rambling is as useless as telling a hopeful writer to study certain well-known fictional characters, without explaining why they were good portrayals or what made them memorable. Uncertain beginners need more specific help.

In the hope of providing it I have drawn up what I believe will be useful guidance. While there are no hard and fast rules and no two authors will work in exactly the same way, there are fundamental issues with which we all have to deal, and the first is undoubtedly the question of bringing characters to life.

I have already stressed that before you can vividly portray imaginary characters you must know them initimately, living with them, letting them thrust themselves into your mind as and when they will. Don't push them, don't chase them; above all, don't be afraid of them. Remember that they are *your* creations; they wouldn't exist but for you, so if anyone can breathe life into them, you can.

Unless a character springs to life as vividly as a charismatic actor onstage, so that from the very first I am strongly aware of them, my own practice is to let them lie fallow in my mind. In this way they become familiar to me. The longer I live with them the more real they usually become, but just occasionally they can prove to be stubborn. When that happens, and if they insist on remaining static, I discard them because they are obviously not going to develop in any helpful way, nor will they prove to be malleable should I attempt to reshape them. Such characters then have to be replaced with others and the whole procedure starts again. That is part of the job and is worth spending time on.

Building character portraits

In the previous chapter I indicated how the hapless theatrical dresser in *The Mating Dance* came to mind after much fruitless searching. The interesting thing was that the unfeeling leading lady presented herself as a contrasting character without any searching at all. I sometimes find that when one character occurs to me another, in complete contrast, follows as a necessary foil. If not, I look for one. This can happen if I stub my toes on a casting problem, such as having too many laudable characters or to many less laudable. An even balance is desirable because it is the characters who give light and shade to a story. Without contrast in looks and personalities, in manners and morals, in behaviour and intelligence, in upbringing and background, a storyteller's pictures will be painted in dull monochrome. Good characterization emerges from the interplay of differing temperaments.

Contrasting characters are therefore not only valuable, but essential. Their very differences set up chain reactions and spur the story forward, so bear in mind that every character, be it in a novel, a short story or a play, must react individually to any situations in which they are involved. It is therefore advisable for an inexperienced writer to know every possible detail about them before starting to write. If characters have not progressed beyond the dummy stage in a writer's mind they won't get very far, and nor will the story.

Although it is true that I never draw up a detailed synopsis (I like to surprise myself as much as my readers) I do jot down notes as characters and situations occur to me even though, when I begin to write, they are almost certain to change. New writers, however, will find complete character dossiers extremely helpful, not only when it comes to character portrayal but in sparking situations which will arise *because* of a character's nature. Detailed pen portraits will register their individual traits, their looks, their idiosyncracies, their backgrounds, their likes and dislikes, their attitudes, their beliefs, and every detail which might otherwise be forgotten. The mere act of recording them will increase your awareness of them and spur your desire to bring them to life.

But don't be surprised if subsidiary characters present themselves along the way, thrusting themselves in as the story develops. This usually happens when you are well launched and is a sure sign that your imagination is working well and that you are writing creatively. They arrive for a purpose, to contribute to the action, so make the most of them. Take stock of them, analyse them and record notes about them so that when they re-enter the story, even after a long lapse of time, they will need no reintroduction because you will have all their characteristics at your finger tips, making them instantly recognisable.

Personal involvement

The most enjoyable part of fiction writing, to me, is becoming involved with a novel as it unfolds, so that I am not only part-creator but part-participator. I am *in* there with my characters and when they 'take over' they carry me with them. When this happens to you, thrust aside any idea that you must force them onto pre-set tracks. Try that, and the exciting, personal contact will be lost and so will be a reader's interest.

At no time must you allow yourself to become a mere puppet-master, jerking the strings. You must bring your characters to life and, at the risk of repetition, I stress again that to do that you must live with them before you even start writing their story. Get to know them and you will find, once you start writing, that their behaviour will come naturally and with little or no prompting from you. Remember what Coleridge said when reviewing *The Mysteries of Udolpho* – 'in the search for what is new, an author is apt to forget what is natural'. In other words, forcing your characters into alien behaviour because you are seeking new and exciting circumstances in which to make them perform, can spell disaster.

How can I best describe the way in which characters 'take over'? It is something that *happens* and you will recognise it and welcome it when it does. Some authors call it 'getting lost in the story', and perhaps that is a fair way of describing it, although the onus of responsibility will still be on you, their creator. You must know your cast so intimately that when one of them starts to behave 'out of character', you are aware of it. When such a situation arises you must overcome it by *looking for the reason*.

Or else a scene suddenly stumbles and, try as you may, you can't rescue it. Invariably, the blame lies not with some*thing* but with some*one*. You have unconsciously allowed a character or characters to behave unnaturally, or have tried to push them in the wrong direction.

This is where your pen portraits come to the rescue. Take out your dossiers, study them carefully and, almost unfailingly, you will realise where, and with whom, the fault lies. You must then go back, scrap the faulty scene and, after reassessment and much thought, re-write from the point at which things began to go wrong, no matter how long it takes. In that way you will get back on the right road and the action will proceed.

Or you may find that the scene fell down at the point where a supplementary character should have been introduced. The arrival of a new face can often help to turn an awkward corner *providing it has a useful part to play, however briefly*. Never forget that even small-part characters, like small-part players onstage, must be as real and convincing as your leads because their minor contributions are just as essential to the story's development.

Actions and reactions

Always remember that the actions and reactions of every person in your story, however important or unimportant, must not only stem from the kind of person they are but, as the story progresses, the kind that they become. People will change in the course of a story, just as they do in real life as a result of their experiences, so you must not only be familiar with them throughout but *understand* them throughout. In this respect, nothing can help you more effectively than your dossiers.

Before you start building up your portrait gallery, however, a note of warning – avoid modelling fictional characters on living people, or on people you know; not even on people with whom you are merely acquainted. Therein can lie danger. Some people are all too eager to identify with fictional characters, especially if they are acquainted with the author and are therefore looking for evidence that they 'have been used'. Despite assertions that people never recognise themselves because their personal idea of what they are like is the reverse of reality, it is not unknown for readers to make claims to the contrary. Such claims have sometimes resulted in libel actions, unpleasant to encounter even when dismissed from the courts.

'I'm afraid of talking to you in case you put me in one of your novels!' The remark was once made to me (somewhat archly) by a woman I scarcely knew. Her fears (or hopes?) were groundless. I find it impossible to base my characters wholly on people I meet. Mannerisms may register and even creep in unconsciously, but never characters as a whole because we can never know people as a whole. We are acquainted only with the personalities they present to the world. This is supported by Graham Greene's admission that he could never model a complex fictional character on a real-life acquaintance because he needed to know much more about the innermost thoughts and feelings of his invented character than he could ever learn about any living person, no matter how close to him the living person might have been.

Nothing could be more true. We all hide certain truths about ourselves even *from* ourselves; truths which we are never able to reveal to others. The inner core of every human being is solitary, and remains so throughout life. That is why everyone craves emotional security which, quite simply, is the desire for love; and love, also very simply, is the vital need to *belong* to someone. You will find, the longer you write, that love in all its varied manifestations, by no means only sexual, is one of the strongest character motivations of all. From it stem countless emotional situations.

Another danger in modelling your fictional characters on real life acquaintances, taking characteristics from here and others from there, is that you will produce very sketchy portraits. Fictional characters need to be portrayed in depth and in the round. This is the object of assembling three-dimensional pictures of your characters. You will be establishing them firmly in your mind from the embryo stage, so start your individual dossiers as each character takes hold of your imagination, even those who are only hazy and who may well remain so; the ineffectual ones whom you may eventually discard. Their presence in your portrait gallery will serve to spotlight the importance of others, on whom you will then focus more attention and who, as a result, will grow 'before your very eyes'.

I suggest you prepare each character dossier along the following lines.

The importance of age

Make particular note of birth dates so that, when writing, you can maintain consistency. This is particularly important when writing a story spanning a number of years, when it is essential that a character should remain at the right age throughout and not be, for instance, twenty-one at the start and thirty-one only five years later.

Noting birth dates will also help you to visualise their growth from childhood and through the progression of time. Even though you may not write of them retrospectively, or refer much to their childhood or youth, you will have a greater depth of feeling for them if you know exactly when they were born and what life was like throughout their formative years, all of which has inevitably left its mark on them.

Remember the importance of age in depicting behaviour. In this it plays as vital a part as physical growth or physical deterioration. (Notice how the voices of older people can become gruffer or more highly pitched, or quavering and breathless.) Remember too that age can influence a person's attitudes, not only to younger people but to life and morals and politics and religion, and that in the young, particularly in teenagers, age can demonstrate itself in boisterous behaviour or shyness, impudence or sulkiness, gaucheness or bravado, defiance or apparently overweaning self-confidence. In the very young, it can reveal a touching dependence on, or trust in, their elders or, in disturbed children, sometimes a fear of them.

Watch children on their way to school; do they go willingly or with feet dragging? Do they run along with others, or walk alone? Watch them, too, in shops or buses. Studying them when out with their parents can be very revealing. How often do you see an obviously united family? How often does the father tag along while the mother is absorbed in the children? Or how often does child walk forlornly while the parents are absorbed in each other?

Degrees of intimacy in personal relationships can be detected even in the most commonplace situations; so, too, can signs of varying ages. Watch out for them and you will be several steps nearer to understanding human nature. Then add the results of your observations to the 'Age' sections of your dossiers.

But remember that behaviour in different periods of time can vary considerably. For example, in an historical novel, particularly a Victorian, the attitude of a young person toward an older one would be one of obedience and respect, no matter what thoughts smouldered beneath. In a modern story the reverse can be true. Parent/child relationships vary from generation to generation. To depict such social changes it is necessary to study the background and level of society against which you are setting your story because authenticity is vital; without it, conviction will be lacking. This is where research comes in, a subject I discuss in more detail in Chapter 10.

The important thing to strive for, when depicting age in relation to behaviour and dialogue, is that it should be typical of the character. Don't, for instance, make him or her behave like a person twenty years younger unless the character itself, such as a woman clinging to her youth, affects such behaviour and mannerisms. If she does, demonstrate them whenever she makes an entrance, but don't overdo them or she will become a bore. A woman forever striving to be young is likely to be a bore anyway, so make the doses minimal. Light touches can convey more than heavy-handed emphasis.

Bear constantly in mind that, whatever a person's age and despite changes due to physical and mental maturity, fundamental characteristics usually remain. Think of people you have known for a long time; try to recall them when younger and compare with the way they are now. They may appear to have changed beyond recognition, but how often, after talking with them, do you think (sometimes with amusement) that he or she 'hasn't changed a bit', they are still blunt and proud of it, or still shy, or still garrulous, or still just that little bit vain.

It will also be useful to realise that in one way age never changes a person and that is in their capacity to be hurt. The belief that 'the torments of youth' cease as people grow older is untrue. Emotions don't become shallower. They become deeper. In preparing a character dossier for an older person, remember that.

Physical attributes

Keep your characters' looks in mind by recording such details as colouring, facial features, blemishes (such as moles and birthmarks), height, weight, and other individual characteristics. Nothing can be too detailed under this heading, for each item will enhance your visual picture. Note skin texture and tone; hair colour and quality – coarse or fine, light or dark, long or short, curly or straight. Note whether a character, particularly female, is likely to ring changes in hairstyles. Note deportment and carriage, speech rhythms, pet slang words, accent or dialect if any, and whether they speak grammatically or ungrammatically, thereby indicating education or lack of it.

Voice tones betray a great deal, and so do gestures and mannerisms. 'Body language' can reveal hyperactivity, agitation, laziness, nervousness, self-assurance, confidence, aggressiveness, shyness, and many other characteristics – but be aware that body language can also be misinterpreted by the inexpert. Poor posture may not be due to awkwardness or clumsiness, but to poor health or physical disability, or even to a lack of confidence resulting from parental criticism or unfavourable comparison with more graceful siblings.

Sitting with eyes downcast, arms tight against the body, glancing quickly at someone and away again, biting worriedly at the lower lip; all can indicate emotional insecurity.

Watch people and make a mental note of such betrayals. Extroverts look around, unafraid of the world. Introverts invariably do not, but nor do shy people who may well come out of their shells when smiled at. You will be able to add much useful material to your physical inventory the more keenly you observe your fellowmen.

Upbringing and environment

Both these factors have a major effect on the formation of character, therefore the more detailed your knowledge of them the stronger will be your character portrayals. You must be aware of every background detail; whether they were brought up in the city or the countryside, in poor homes or otherwise, happy or unhappy – and what made them so.

What were their parents like? Was *their* marriage a warm and united one or did it break up, with an adverse effect on family life? How many brothers and sisters were there, and were they affectionate or quarrelsome and antagonistic? What sort of an education did your characters have, particularly your main one? Did he or she rebel against schooling, or grow up with an unrequited thirst for knowledge? If so, why, in both cases? What of childhood dreams and traumas – what caused them? And what about childhood successes and failures, both of which can have a lifetime's effect and be responsible for future happiness or unhappiness? These are only some of the environmental influences from which your characters will grow, finally emerging as complete people, wholly convincing.

You must not only be aware of your leading character's unbringing and background, but of those of friends and relations even if those friends and relations never enter your story. They will be alive in your main character's mind, and through his or her mind you will come to know them, so concentrate on those who played an important part in their developing years. To focus on one in particular, as Emlyn Williams focused on the school mistress in *The Corn is Green*, or as Muriel Spark did in *The Prime of Miss Jean Brodie*, can be tremendously productive. From such characters a whole story can grow, authentic in detail and background, richly alive.

Marital status, or lack of it, is always important. On it can hinge the development of many emotional scenes. Similarly, career history and resultant ambitions can play vital parts both actively and emotionally.

Think deeply about every aspect of your character's upbringing until the details become as real to you as the details of your own life. You are unlikely to incorporate all such details in your script – to do so could overburden your story – but their influence will be powerful. This is their value to you. They are the colours you will use to paint a more vivid picture, bringing your characters strongly to life.

Religious influences

Religion may not play a part in your story, but you should still take into account its possible effect on a character's personality. A religious background, or lack of it, can colour their development. The influence of a devout family could prevail into adulthood, or wane and then reassert itself in later years, whereas the influence of a bigotted or fanatically religious unbringing has been known to drive a person toward atheism. Religious influence and conflict featured powerfully in Graham Greene's works, and were the main theme in Susan Howatch's *Glittering Images* and its sequels.

Sexuality

It is important to know whether your character is sexually experienced or not. The influence of sexuality on character development, and therefore on behaviour and action within the plot, is something you should be aware of even if you don't introduce sex scenes. It is important because sexuality influences attitudes toward other people. It is a vital underlying instinct which has a profound effect on a personality.

As you build up your files you will want to add more categories, such as career, vocation, hobbies, skills, interests, even though you may finally use little of the information stored there. It is nonetheless important to familiarize yourself with as much detail as possible because such knowledge increases your intimacy with your characters. It brings them to life in your mind. Now your job is to bring them to life on the page.

But before you start, a final plea, bear in mind that a wholly good person is a rarity so, to make them human, give your 'good' characters some flaws and your 'bad' characters some saving graces. The physical and moral perfection attributed to heroes prior to World War Two, in women's fiction particularly, along with the thoroughly-bad-cad as his opposite number, were as untrue to life as the beautiful and saintly heroine who never failed to win the handsome hero, not to mention the badder-than-bad-bitch who always got her come-uppence. After the war the market for boy-meets-girl-and-stop-at-the-bedroom-door type of fiction rapidly died. The anti-hero was born and the unglamorous, but mercifully normal, heroine made her welcome entry.

So if you are aiming for the romantic genre, give your heroine some realistic imperfections, both physical and psychological, with which women readers can identify, and give her rival some likeable character-istics which will win some sympathy. And do the same for your hero and villain. Then, at least, your quartet will be human.

5
Motivation

Making your characters tick

When a story is rejected as 'implausible' it is immediately assumed that this refers to the plot, whereas the implausibility is more likely to be in character motivation, rendering the whole thing unconvincing.

The reason why the bizarre plots of successful fantasy and horror writers are so popular is because the authors motivate their characters *believably*, making the books plausible and therefore acceptable. It matters little to their readers that in real life such stories could not be true although, as with well written science fiction, it is always wondered whether they just *might* be, but true devotees of fantasy and horror accept the plots without question, enjoying the thrills and chills.

But would they if the writing and characterization were weak? In the case of Dean Koontz the prose is literary, in Stephen King's it holds a style of its own, and in both cases the plots grip because the motivation of their characters is believable.

Put the plots of Ira Levin's *The Stepford Wives* and *Rosemary's Baby* under the microscope (and even *The Boys From Brazil* although cloning has now been established as a possibility) and both will appear to be bizarre and unbelievable, but their success is the result of convincing character motivation.

This essential applies to the whole spectrum of popular fiction, whatever the genre. The motivation behind your characters' behaviour will make them either convincing or unconvincing and your book acceptable or unacceptable.

Differing motivations

What are the strongest, and the most common, motivations?

First: **Love**. Too many people give a faint curl of the lip if you admit to writing romance. One would almost think it was an obscene word, yet love is a universal and vital emotion and scarcely a successful novel, whatever the field of literature, does not feature it. Throughout the ages authors and dramatists and poets have written about love more than they have written about any other human emotion. Shakespeare used it as powerful motivation in *Romeo and Juliet*, and included it in nearly all his plays, from *Twelfth Night*, *A Midsummer Night's Dream*, *The Taming of the Shrew*, and *Antony and Cleopatra*, to *King Lear* where the emphasis was on filial devotion. Dickens included it, in all its aspects, in novels which, in his lifetime, were regarded as pulp for the masses but which have now achieved immortality as classics, even though his characters were larger than life and his prose often flamboyant. His books, because of his skill in characterization and his understanding of motivation, live on.

Love as a motivation is by no means confined to Mills & Boon romances. It was vital in Daphne du Maurier's *Rebecca*, an (almost) Cinderella story elevated to the ranks of accepted literature by stylish writing, excellence of plot, good atmosphere, vivid background, and strongly motivated characters. She also used it with great finesse in her swashbuckling adventure tale, *Frenchman's Creek*. Evelyn Anthony's espionage novels succeed not only because of plot intricacies but because of her deep understanding of, and compassion for, human nature. She uses love movingly and dramatically in books like *The Assassin*, *The Malaspega Exit*, *The Tamarind Seed*, and heart-rendingly in *The Rendezvous*. Read any of these books and you will realise the value of love, happy or tragic, as character motivation.

Love has also been, and will for ever be, an inspiration to poets and an unending theme for popular songs. Pop stars have grown rich from singing about it and the Brontës, from the depths of their repressed lives, wrote about it with passion. Dumas, Sabatini, George Eliot, Nathaniel Hawthorne, Thomas Hardy and other classical authors introduced it, in all its varied forms, into their works.

Each and every one of us wants to love and be loved. A supportive human relationship is the need of us all. Your readers are the same. Use love as a motivation and you will win their interest, and hold it.

Although love can be one of the most powerful motivations and can be adapted in one form or another to any kind of plot (even to crime – how about the *crime passionnel*?), the dewy-eyed romantic variety can usually serve only the most novelettish of stories. Like all motivations, it needs the support of others to give it strength and impact. **Self-sacrifice** is one; the self-sacrifice of a wife for a husband or a husband for a wife, of a mother for her child, of a father for his family. There are plenty of permutations on this theme and Dickens used it well in *A Tale of Two Cities*, 'It is a far, far better thing that I do, than I have ever done . . .' said Sydney Carton as he went voluntarily to the guillotine in place of Charles Darnay because he loved the man's wife.

This demonstrates that one type of motivation alone will not necessarily suffice. Invariably, it needs strengthening with another.

Combining motivations

Below is a list of other motivations which can combine with, or spring from, each other. It is by no means definitive and can be added to with a little thought.

Greed
Jealousy
Revenge
Duty
Fear
Vanity
Hatred
Loneliness

Let's take the first. **Greed** is an unattractive motivation to attribute to an heroic leading character, but if he were the anti-hero so popular today, say a ruthless freedom fighter determined to steal funds to spike a military government's guns and free his people, it could win a reader's sympathy. Or if he were a hard-up daredevil diving for sunken treasure which, despite the law, he fully intends to keep in order to marry the girl he loves, the reader would be half won over, and completely so were there a well-heeled rival lacking the need or the inclination to risk his neck and self-satisfied into the bargain. The portrayal of such a rival would thrust sympathy fairly and squarely on the rogue hero, his greed forgiven. Readers would even be rooting for his success.

Again, the secret of making such a quality acceptable is to combine it with some nobler motive, but it would also be made understandable in a man who has risen from nothing, worked hard at his trade and established his own successful business at long last, only to discover that a life-long friend has swindled him on a vast scale and brought him to bankruptcy. **Revenge** would then be the key motivation, a determination not only to get back every penny but to get it with added interest (there greed comes in) and to ruin the man in return. Add to this the fact that the life-long friend has also stolen his wife, and you are plunged into the additional motivations of **Hatred** and **Jealousy**. You immediately have a more deeply drawn and interesting character, and one very true to life.

By showing readers the *reasons* for a person's behaviour, whether noble or reprehensible, you will paint a more vivid picture. Look at the pen-portrait you have drawn of him, turn to his background details, find the childhood influences or the adverse upbringing which moulded him, and through your greater understanding you will portray him with sympathy, and he will live.

Now, as an exercise, see what you can do with **Duty**, **Fear**, **Vanity** and **Loneliness**. These by no means represent all human motivations, but the vast majority of us are certainly familiar with them, with the possible exception of the first, duty, which was more strongly emphasized in earlier times than it is today, when unquestioning service to king and country and, sometimes, even to parents and families, has diminished. To associate duty with a period figure may therefore be an easier choice, though to focus on the carers of today (for whom public sympathy is rightly increasing) could be an acceptable angle.

Or take loneliness combined with fear. To me, this immediately suggests a contemporary scene; an old lady too terrified to emerge from her high-rise flat in a voilent city area. You could get a scalp-tingling short story out of such a situation if you put yourself thoroughly into the character.

Combining vanity with fear immediately conjures up a beautiful but unhappy woman and her fear of aging, of losing her looks, of no longer being admired or wanted; fear that her husband is being unfaithful with someone younger; fear of widowhood and loneliness. This is wonderful material for characterization, bringing so many other motivations into play; resentment, suspicion, bitterness, even slowly corroding hatred of the world and of life.

Think about her and then start writing about her. Your own interpretation will be quite different, bearing your own individual stamp.

As another exercise take a character not only known to millions of TV viewers but once heading the popularity stakes despite being a thoroughly reprehensible type – J.R. Ewing. He displayed all the flaws any man could possibly be endowed with yet he stood out in that long-running soap opera as the most memorable figure of all. J.R.'s believability was not merely due to Larry Hagman's acting, but to the authors' thorough motivation of his character. List those motivations for yourself. Draw your own pen-portrait of him; line up his background, his childhood, his attitudes to others. Plainly, he was jealous of his younger brother, but what made him so? Was he compared unfavourably with him in boyhood? Did girls find Bobby more physically attractive and only want J.R. when he became head of Ewing Oil? What deep-rooted influences produced his ruthlessness and his callous attitude to women?

I don't know whether J.R.'s earlier life was ever revealed, but it would seem to have been cushioned against discomfort. Create this earlier life for yourself. What was the influence of his father, or of the ever-patient and homely M's Ellie? Did he become the school bully, and if so, why? Probe into his past, analyse his character, decide what made him tick and why such a man could win the public's sympathy. You will find endless motivations beneath the complexities of J.R.'s character and then you will know what made it so believable.

But don't use him in any story you propose to sell. He still belongs to the script writers who created him, so any character inspired by him must be wholly new, as I stressed in Chapter 2.

Finally, take all the motivations I listed and add to them. Start applying them to your pen-portraits and your anxiety about bringing characters to life will diminish. You will be creating *live* characters of your own and be ready to go on to the next contributory factor – dialogue.

6
Dialogue

Natural v unnatural

It is frequently said that fiction should be the mirror of reality, but this is true only up to a point. Fiction is really the essence of reality distilled into an assimilable form. The same is true of fictional dialogue, which beginners are constantly urged to write as naturally as possible, but if we were to conceal a tape recorder when two or three people were in 'natural' conversation the result would be a mass of superflous words, irrelevancies, repetitions, interruptions, contradictions, unfinished sentences and disjointed phrases, all of which, if reproduced for the printed page, would be rambling and pointless, defeating its aim. That aim, as with narrative, should be to advance the story.

The following passage of 'natural' dialogue illustrates what I mean. Two married couples meeting in a coffee shop could sound something like this:

'Hello there, you two! How are you? Oh damn, I forgot to get skin cream in Boots! I'd better go back – no, I'll do it later, I'm *dying* for coffee – no, p'raps I'd better go right away or I might forget again. . . .'

'Sit down and stop dithering, Mabel. Women!'

'Janet's just the same, old chap. Makes a shopping list and then forgets it. Stinking day, isn't it?'

'Bloody awful.'

'How's the election going down your way?'

'Dunno. Haven't heard.'

'Now don't let's have any politics! Men! It's either that or cricket. Black, please – no sugar. Jan, I – *must* show you the bra I picked up in that new little French shop! Oh, I *do* wish I hadn't forgotten that skin cream!'

'How's the Test Match going, George? Missed it on the telly.'

'This coffee's too strong. Call the girl, Bill.'

'"*She's either too hot or too cold . . . She's either too strong or too bold . . .*" I'll bet that doesn't apply to the pretty one, eh, George? OK, love, I'm calling her.'

'Your husband's very chirpy this morning.'

'Isn't he just! Oh, while I think of it, I *must* tell you what happened at the Women's Institute. Hilda Turner fairly *spat* because she didn't get on the committee or counsel or whatever they call it. . . .'

'Thank goodness she didn't! Grace Walker'd be better, look at all the jam she makes. Heavens, you're not going to *wear* that, are you? It's not decent!'

'Well, George likes it. Fetching, he calls it. And I haven't lost my figure yet.'

'Know what *I* think, Bill? They oughta get Gower back.'

'Botham. That's who they need.'

'There they go, cricket again! Well, *I* don't like Grace Walker's jam and she always makes such a *thing* about it, showing off and all that, as if no other woman ever made any. Why d'you call it indecent? Jealous?'

'Listen to 'em. Women!'

'They oughta get Gower back.'

'Y'know, I think I will go back to Boots. . . .'

'Botham's the man.'

'Well, I *like* Grace Walker's jam . . .'

And so *ad infinitum*.

You can overhear conversations like that all too frequently and you could write continuously in that vein without getting anywhere or revealing much about the speakers except, in this case, that one wife is scatterbrained, the other a bit strait-laced, and both husbands are bores. Such idle chit-chat would hinder rather than advance the action of a story, so let's leave those pedestrian people to their rambling repetitiveness and embark on a scene featuring more useful fictional dialogue.

Let's imagine that a woman is worried about her husband's behaviour. He has become uncommunicative, watchful, his manner guarded. On the surface and in the presence of others he is his normal self, but when alone his attitude changes. She feels threatened by it, particularly since she has recently received menacing 'phone calls in an unrecognisable voice; calls which began shortly after her tycoon father died and she inherited his wealth. When telling her husband about the anonymous calls, he had laughed and called her neurotic, but now he is insisting that she needs long term psychiatric help. ('It's well known that women of a certain age can fantasize. You haven't been imagining those 'phone calls again, I hope?') She avoids telling him that, far from imagining them, she is still receiving them and that she suspects the voice to be deliberately muffled, because the more she thinks about it the more she fears that it is his.

But what reason could he have?

A very good one. She has control of her inherited wealth so long as she is in good health and of sound mind, otherwise that control passes to her husband, and the recession has hit his business badly.

After weeks of increasing tension, she is desperate to talk to someone. She thinks of her friends, Sylvia and Peter, who live nearby and whom she trusts. Even so, she feels self-conscious when ringing their doorbell, also somewhat guilty because surely no loyal wife would accuse her husband of treachery?

The following approach to the scene would be natural in real life, but overwritten for fiction.

> Ruth paused, her finger on the bell push. It was absurd to feel so nervous. After all, they were her personal friends more than they were Ralph's, she and Sylvia having grown up together. She could trust them; they would listen with sympathy and understanding. She found herself insisting on that in her mind.
>
> Sylvia answered the door.
>
> 'Ruth, my dear! How lovely to see you! I was saying to Peter only today that I haven't seen you all week.' She held the door wide. 'Come along in. How are you? And Ralph, how's he?'
>
> 'Fine. Well – we're both fine, really.'
>
> Closing the door, Sylvia said, 'What d'you mean – "really"? One of you been a bit off colour? Is that why we haven't seen you at the golf club?'
>
> Ruth was glad to follow her into the pleasant living room overlooking the garden. Peter was fiddling with the video. 'I want him to record the new Inspector Morse,' Sylvia said. 'It's on at nine and we'll be out – Mother's birthday, so of course we must be there.' Peter was absorbed, so his wife tapped him on the shoulder. 'Darling – Ruth's here. How about drinks?'
>
> 'Ruth! Nice to see you. Just a tick . . . There, that's it.' Peter rose, kissed Ruth's cheek affectionately and headed for the sideboard. 'What'll you have? The usual?'
>
> 'I – I don't think I fancy anything – '
>
> Caught by the bleak note in her voice, Sylvia said in concern, 'Is something wrong? I thought you looked a bit peaked when I opened the door.'
>
> 'Off colour?' asked Peter. 'That's not like you, Ruthie. You're always the picture of blooming health. Here, get this down. It'll do you good.'
>
> But his wife was more perceptive. '*Is* something wrong?'
>
> 'As a matter of fact, yes.' Ruth hesitated. 'You'll think I've taken leave of my senses, but – well – I've got to talk to *some*one and you two have been my friends for so long. . . .'

All to often we linger over preliminaries and exchange pleasantries before getting down to serious conversation, but in fiction such extended dialogue would hold up the action (it could also tempt readers to skip a page or two) so for fiction we must prune it and get to the point.

Like this?

> Ruth wasted no time in ringing the doorbell and, to her relief, Sylvia wasted no time in answering it.
>
> 'Sylvia!' Ruth gasped. 'You've got to help me! Ralph's trying to have me put away. I'm terrified!'

No, not like that. That's jumping the gun. Let's write it again, bearing in mind that we must convey the essence and the emotion of the conversation without elaboration.

> Ruth was glad when Sylvia promptly answered the door. It gave her no time to hesitate or withdraw.
>
> 'Ruth! How nice to see you! Come along in. I was thinking of you only today.' She drew her friend inside, glancing at her in concern. 'Is something wrong? You don't look too good.'
>
> 'I'm all right – just worried. No. Frightened. I – I thought perhaps I could talk it over with you and Peter, though I expect you'll think I'm imagining things – '
>
> 'Now why should we think that?'
>
> 'Because it sounds insane to say that Ralph is trying to have me put away.' She reached out, seized her friend's hands, and clung to them. 'But that's what I believe . . .!'

Examine those examples while bearing in mind the golden rule that dialogue should advance a story as effectively as a slice of narrative action, and you will recognise that the first passage served no useful purpose because it dawdled amiably before coming to the point; in fact, if you look at it again you will see that even by the last line it did not actually reach it. The second failed because it rushed ahead to make some dramatic impact and resulted in being abrupt and melodramatic, proving that to over-compress dialogue can be as ineffective as overburdening it. The third was acceptable because it distilled the scene to its essentials, yet retained the emotion. It also cut out Peter's ineffective contribution (though he could play an effective part later) and clearly indicated Ruth's nervous tension, also her relief because she was given no time to heed her instinct to run away.

Tension was also indicated by her reaching for Sylvia's hands and clinging to them. In addition, her friend's sympathetic character was revealed in her immediate perception of Ruths anxiety, and finally emotion plus fear were brought to a head when Ruth blurted out the truth. The action was not only ready to move on, but had taken a vital step forward.

How much dialogue to include?

Claims have been made that few novels are bought that contain less than 20 to 40 per cent of dialogue, but such claims are confounded by many highly successful and well written novels, amongst which the Raj novels of Paul Scott spring to mind, as do the crime novels of P.D. James, whose narrative prose is as alive and as telling as her dialogue and enjoyable to read because of its literary quality. It is this literary quality that elevates her books above the majority of crime fiction, but only with time and experience will the *average* beginner reach such a degree of expertise, and note that I stress the word 'average' because natural-born writers producing outstanding first novels are certainly not unknown. They are, however, in the minority. The vast majority of aspiring authors achieve a high degree of professionalism only through the qualities I named in my opening chapter, dedication, hard work, and enthusiasm. In addition to these essentials they must develop an ear for dialogue.

One good way of doing this is to study not only the works of successful novelists, but of notable playwrights too. Such plays can be obtained from local libraries and good bookshops.

Reading stage dialogue can be not only enjoyable, but instructive. Start with plays like Ira Levin's *Death Trap* and you will see how every spoken line advances the action, reveals character, and helps to create tension and atmosphere. In fiction, dialogue must do the same.

The dialogue tag

When reading novels by skilled authors, notice how little they rely on dialogue tags; 'he said', 'she said', and so on. When two people are in conversation no such tags should be necessary. One person speaks and the other answers, so if you have established who speaks first, there will be a natural interchange and the reader will easily identify each speaker. Differential is also established by presenting every line of dialogue as a new paragraph, as in the following interchange between Joseph Boswell and his illegitimate daughter in *The Mating Dance*.

The daughter is facing her father the morning after a late return from the theatre. Her face bears signs of injury. (The book is written in first-person singular, the girl telling the story.)

'I hope Gavin Calder was not responsible?'
'Gavin! He would never hurt me.'
'Then were you attacked on your way home? Surely you didn't return on foot? You know I will never permit that.'

'We came by hansom, as always, and I suffered no violence anywhere, in any way. I tripped over an angle rod backstage and hurt my face. That's all.'

I was now anxious to change the subject; anxious for him to be gone. I wanted no questions about last night.

He said thoughtfully, 'That is what you want me to believe.'

'It is the truth.'

'No. You are hiding something from me, but because it's your wish I will accept your story. Your mother is another matter. She must be cared for.'

'The Steels are doing that. We're remaining with them until I can make other arrangements.'

'*You* make other arrangements, a girl barely sixteen!'

'I can find employment.'

'You have it already.'

'A minor player doesn't earn enough for what I intend to do.'

He became angry.

'You heard me say last night that you and Trudy are my responsibility and that I will make arrangements for both of you. I insist on that.'

'I don't consider you have the right.'

'I claim it. I'll find a home for both of you and you will have the career you were intended for. You will justify the ability you have inherited from me and fulfil all my ambitions for you.' His tone changed. 'I beg you not to disappoint me in this.'

'Surely you don't imagine I could come back to the theatre and continue as a member of the company? There would be embarrassment all round, and besides, Lady Boswell would never agree.'

'It is I who owns the Boswell Theatre and the Boswell Company, and don't forget you have a contract for that part, small though it is. I shall keep you to it. Only the management can terminate a contract, never a player. To enable you to earn more money, you can also understudy the part of Lucie.'

I refused point blank. 'First my mother as your wife's shadow, and now I as your daughter's? Never.'

'That's not how I think of either you or Trudy.'

'It is how *I* would feel.'

And now read the same interchange with dialogue tags. To save time we will pick up the scene half way:

'It is the truth!' I declared vehemently.

'No,' he answered emphatically. 'You are hiding something from me, but because it's your wish I will accept your story. Your mother is another matter. She must be cared for.'

'The Steels are doing that. We're remaining with them until I can make other arrangements,' I retorted triumphantly.

'*You* make other arrangements!' he expostulated. 'A girl barely sixteen!'

'I can find employment,' I flung at him.

'You have that already,' he pointed out angrily.

'A minor player doesn't earn enough for what I intend to do,' I told him resolutely.

At that he became angry. 'You heard me say last night that you and Trudy are my responsibility and that I will make arrangements. I insist on that,' he raged.

'I don't consider you have the right,' I retorted cruelly.

'I claim it,' he shouted furiously. . . .

And so on, and so on. An editor would have been itching to delete all those surplus dialogue tags and, if you have managed to read the revised version to the end, you will have been irritated by the unnecessary identification of each speaker and by the repetitive use of adverbs to describe voice tones.

Many new writers wrongly imagine that to use elaborate dialogue tags gives a 'literary' tone to their writing – words like 'ejaculated', 'expostulated', 'protested', 'gasped', 'choked', 'queried', 'probed', 'avowed', 'declared', 'exclaimed' – the list is endless and all are not only unnecessary but irritating because they upset the rhythm of the dialogue and therefore jar. They also make a laboured job of the writing and, in consequence, heavy reading.

Remember that words should speak for themselves, as they did in the first passage, and that the meaning can be enhanced with correct punctuation. Why use the word 'exclaimed' when an exclamation mark indicates this? Or 'asked' when a question mark serves the same function? Or 'protested' and 'declared' when the words themsleves are clearly words of protest or declaration?

When you are writing dialogue between more than two people, conditions are slightly different. You will, when necessary, have to indicate who is speaking, particularly when interruptions occur or newcomers join in. Therefore the use of a certain amount of dialogue tags will be unavoidable, but use them only when essential and don't waste time in searching for synonyms to replace unobtrusive words like 'said' and 'asked'. Remember too that readers are intelligent enough to interpret dialogue for themselves. There is no need to strive after effect in order to impress them, or to feel that you have to emphasize every tone of voice. Stick to the minimum of dialogue tags, and the most simple, and they will not intrude.

Similarly, avoid the over-use of adverbs. Some new writers tend to scatter them like confetti . . . 'he shouted jubilantly', 'she cried delightedly', 'they protested vigorously', 'he exploded furiously'. The words uttered by your characters should express delight or fury or vigorous protest, or whatever emotion prompts them, without any need for description. Similarly, too many adjectives describing nouns are superfluous and undesirable.

Resist the temptation to 'make up a chorus from *Roget's Thesaurus'*. If you do, no one is going to be impressed by your literary expertise.

Direct and indirect dialogue

Creating well balanced dialogue, i.e. between the direct and indirect, is a question of technique and need not be frightening.

Direct dialogue is used when one character tells another about certain events, as in the scene where Ruth related her fear and suspicion to Sylvia.

Indirect dialogue would then be used when Sylvia told Peter. This device is employed when the reader already knows the details and repetition would be not only unnecessary but would make the reader wonder why it was being repeated yet again.

To demonstrate, let's cut into that scene between Ruth and Sylvia and then continue with it, utilising both direct and indirect dialogue:

Example 1: Direct Dialogue:
  '. . . Because it sounds insane to say that my husband is trying to have me put away . . .' She reached out and clung to her friend's hands. 'But that is what I believe!'
  'My dear – he *wouldn't*! Whatever makes you think such a thing?'
  'He insists that I need a psychiatrist. "Long term psychiatry", he says. I know what that means and it terrifies me. So do the 'phone calls I've been getting. He swears I imagine them. The awful thing is that they're in *his* voice . . . muffled . . .'

The last paragraph continued in direct dialogue because it was necessary for Ruth to relate the circumstances to Sylvia, her friend being in ignorance, and it would be acceptable to readers, though already aware of the facts, because they would be interested to know precisely how she would confide in her friend, and how her friend would react, thereby extending the drama. However, if Sylvia then drew Ruth into the living room where Peter was fiddling with the video, repetition would be undesirable. It would therefore be necessary to write the scene like this:

Example 2: Indirect Dialogue:
  'Darling – Ruth's here.' Sylvia stooped and tapped her husband on

the shoulder. 'Could you leave that for now? There's something serious
. . . something you must hear . . .'

Sensing his wife's concern, Peter looked up. At the sight of Ruth's
white face, he quietly reached for the brandy.

'Tell me,' he said.

While he poured, Sylvia repeated what Ruth had told her.

The final line is indirect dialogue.

On the whole, direct dialogue is preferable to indirect except in the
following cases:

(a)   When a character must repeat information to another which has
already been imparted in direct dialogue. (As in *Example 2*.)

(b)   When a character must explain to another something the reader
does not have to learn in detail, such as how to operate a machine of
some kind. (. . . *She showed the new secretary how to operate the
word processor. . . .*) Detailed instructions would not enthral the
reader, nor would they advance the action. Unless the word processor
plays a necessary part in the plot, it may only be there to add to the
description of an office background, in which case the mechanics are
unimportant.

(c)   When long passages of direct dialogue could be broken up,
shortened, or lightened by the injection of a few lines of indirect
dialogue, such as in a scene where a detective is making a verbal report
about a case. (. . . *He told Lord William how Lady Dorothy had been
traced to Bournemouth, and the circumstances in which she was
living with the reprobate Clive Anderson . . .*) The advantages of
indirect dialogue are particularly useful in such scenes.

Both direct and indirect dialogue can be used to break up the sort of
denouément scene popular in crime fiction, where the amateur sleuth
describes to an assembled company exactly how the crime was com-
mitted. Questions in direct dialogue could be interchanged with lines
of indirect dialogue, such as: *The Colonel asked how he first came to
suspect the murderer*, then back to the sleuth's revelations in direct
dialogue.

Revealing character through dialogue

Up to a point, we reveal ourselves to others whenever we speak. We
reveal our thoughs and our moods, our knowledge or lack of it, our
sense of humour and our personalities. If we have regional accents, we
reveal where we come from. Even our silences can betray us. How

many times have you guessed what someone was thinking when they stubbornly (or wisely) refused to speak?

Turn to your dossiers and renew your acquaintance with your characters, then put words into their mouths and listen to them speak. If your pen portraits are realistic you will know how they think and how they talk. You will know that, as a general rule, the more educated are likely to speak accordingly, but not necessarily with greater confidence because much depends on their individual natures and the circumstances of their lives. Example: A younger son can feel decidedly inferior to an elder brother, and a daughter can be overshadowed by a beautiful or successful mother. In both instances, though they may have had the finest educations in the world, they may lack self-confidence.

Pay attention to speech rhythms, pet slang words, accents and dialects, but don't overdo them. Individual verbal quirks will help to register your characters, not only in your own mind, but in your reader's, so that it will only be necessary to introduce touches to make them instantly recognisable.

This is how dialogue helps you to bring characters to life. Let them speak for themselves. Don't force words into their mouths just because you consider them to be clever or witty. The chances are that they may be wholly inappropriate and therefore sound false or unnatural.

Finally, as an exercise, write a dialogue scene between Ruth and her husband Ralph, bringing out his veiled cruelty and her fear and suspicion of him, then as a follow-up exercise write a dialogue scene between Sylvia, Ruth and Peter. When you have written both, read them aloud or record them on tape and play them back. Both are excellent ways in which to get your ear attuned to acceptable dialogue.

Now ask yourself this two-part question: Does the dialogue in either scene merely mark time, like that between the quartet in the coffee shop, or does it advance the story? If you can truthfully answer 'No' to the first and 'Yes' to the second, you are on your way to recognising, and ultimately writing, good fictional conversation.

7
Style and Viewpoint

What is style?

According to many textbooks on the craft of writing, style is a question of approach – first person, third, or ominiscient – but part of a lengthy Oxford English Dictionary definition is '. . . manner of writing, speaking, or doing . . . collective characteristics of writing or diction or artistic expression or way of presenting things . . . in the manner of Shakspeare, Raphael, Wagner. . . .' None of which teaches us much, except a new way of spelling the Bard's name!

In any case you, the aspiring author with common sense, are not aiming to be the second 'Shakespeare' or the second anybody. Your aim is to be the first You, so that when someone picks up a novel or short story written by you they will recognise your style at once.

Most new authors overwrite. The thought of cutting their work shocks them. All those dedicated hours, all that laboured effort, all that deathless prose laid to waste! The thought is positively painful, yet a vast percentage of popular fiction written by aspiring authors could be improved and made marketable by a courageous application of the 'blue pencil'.

The keynote of readability is simplicity. Bog down your reader with over-written narrative and a mass of obscure words and your book will be put aside. Bear in mind that your function as a story teller is to entertain your reader, and how can you do that if you can't tell the story with ease? By that I don't mean casual and slip-shod writing; I mean the kind of prose that is simple and direct and seems deceptively easy to write, but there was never a truer saying than 'easy reading is damned hard writing'.

One of the finest exponents of this style was Ernest Hemingway. Read *The Old Man and The Sea*. It contains not one over-elaborate sentence yet it ranks among the greats.

I am not saying that good prose should not contain vivid metaphors or similes (though the simile needs to be good if it is not to appear contrived), but if a novel contains so many that they occur in every other paragraph the style can become wearisome and act as an obstacle to readability. Nor, in contrast, am I saying that your fiction should be as precise as journalism which, even at its best, is written mainly for factual communication. Nor am I saying that novels containing clichés, contrived similes, and laboured metaphors don't get published. We have all, at some time or another, struggled to read such books and put them aside.

What I *am* saying is: Don't handicap your novel by trying to be clever, or trying to impress some unknown reader with your vocabulary and your skill in using it. In the process you may well lose sight of your main objective: to tell a story. Bear in mind that your job, as a novelist, is to do precisely that and the more simply and directly you do it the more readable you will be.

Approach, ancient and modern

Since approach is an important part of style, let's now examine the three main ones, starting with the omniscient.

In this style you play God, talking down to your readers, forecasting what is to come, writing in the present tense and introducing your characters almost with a running commentary accompanied by interjections and much sermonising. The Victorians loved it and presented it in this way:

> Amelia hurries down the darkening lane, clutching her sweeping skirts in one trembling hand and her valise in the other, her guilty heart racing in time with her frantic steps. Oh, how wicked she has been to run away! Such behaviour is always disgraceful in a well brought up young lady, as you and I know, gentle reader. She must now go back and face whatever penance her sin so rightly deserves, but alas, she has lost her way and gathering fog now obscures her vision! Then suddenly her heart lifts, for out of the darkness looms the shadow of a house. Oh, merciful promise of shelter on this woeful night! But poor Amelia is mistaken. Little does she dream of what lies ahead. Pity her, dear reader, for the shock and distress in store, and pray that courage will sustain her.

You may argue that no author writes that way today, but many aspiring ones touch the fringe of it. Unconsciously, they adapt it to modern thought and idiom, often retaining the present tense so popular with the Victorians. Study the next example and you will see what I mean.

> The car engine splutters, dies, and refuses to come alive. Furiously, Martin seizes his suitcase and begins to walk. He feels guilty for slamming the door on his parents after the row about his association with Ruby. Just because she'd been divorced twice didn't mean there would

be a third time. All the same, he should not have behaved like that. He must go back and talk over the whole thing reasonably and quietly. He must make amends, as his regrettable behaviour so rightly demands, for no son should treat his parents in such a fashion.

The breakdown of his car is frustrating, but he recalls driving over a level crossing a short time ago, which means that a train service should not be too far distant. And he is right – or so he thinks. He can see a huddle of buildings which he takes to be a station, but little does he dream how wrong he is. It would have been wiser to search for a garage to repair his car, but of course he does not know that yet. Nor can he envisage the nightmare lying in wait for him.

This foreshadowing of events may be preferable to the rambling writing of earlier days, but it still jars and the author's interjections and sermonising are not only obtrusive but irritating.

Such a style is unacceptable today. It can be called 'the seeing eye' or the 'judicial omniscient', both of which make for bad writing and worse reading. Even so, varied samples continue to land on the desks of fiction editors, usually in travel-weary typescripts.

Enough of the omniscient, seeing-eye and foreshadowing styles, and on to the next logical step.

Third person 'limited' and third person 'straight'

In some ways third person 'limited' can be an extension of the omniscient, but with no interpolations, no sermonising, and no stage asides. The author writes from a grandstand seat, but he is not there to make a commentary so again his voice must never be heard. Because he stays with the main character throughout, usually the hero or heroine, he relates the story entirely from that character's point of view, thus limiting it. It is a device to win exclusive sympathy for the leading character.

This single minded approach is akin to the normal (or 'straight') third person, but is much more restrictive. In the latter the author ostensibly focuses on the central character, but has the advantage of getting within the skin of all other characters and moving with them from scene to scene instead of remaining doggedly with the hero. He is therefore able to present their thoughts and actions as well as the leading character's. This form of third person approach is a popular method of storytelling and therefore the most used, but it has its dangers as well as its advantages.

Apart from the advantage of being able to switch from character to character and from place to place, there is the advantage of being able to open a new scene with a different person each time, or resurrecting one who bowed out earlier but who can now be useful in engineering a dramatic turn in events. This gives the author a welcome breather and avoids the likelihood of being stuck in a rut, wondering how to get out of it. It also enables him to reveal off-stage behaviour and dialogue, *but* it also lures an inexperienced writer into one specific danger, that of leaping from the thoughts and actions of one character to another in scenes which should focus only on the character occupying centre stage.

Jumping from character to character and from mind to mind *within a scene* will destroy that scene. Here is an example:

> As James paced the floor, waiting for Helen to arrive, he was conscious of the threadbare carpet, the shabby room, the spluttering gas fire which indicated that the fifty pence he had put in the meter was running out and, dear God, what would he do if it ran out completely and the room was frozen by the time she came? He couldn't spare another fifty so soon. As for his shoes, he hoped the polish he had diligently applied would disguise their shabbiness and that the careful pressing he had given his suit would do the same. It would be galling if she were to guess how things were with him now.
>
> When he opened the door, she stared. She looked beyond him to the depressing bed-sitter. She saw the cheap curtains and the stained wall-paper. She could even detect a sort of fading, gassy smell as if one of those awful spluttery things was on the point of going out. And as for James . . . his cuffs were frayed and his shoes shabby. He looked down on his luck. Well, well, well . . . who'd have expected James to sink to this?
>
> James smiled nervously. He knew what she was thinking. He wished she had never traced him. He felt humiliated and ashamed and hated her for it. He wanted to tell her to go. He wanted to slam the door in her face. He couldn't. He could only stand aside for her to enter.

I wrote that to demonstrate how continuity can be destroyed by switching from the inside of James's mind (paragraph one) to the inside of Helen's (paragraph two) and back again to James's (paragraph three). The whole scene should have been enacted through *his* mind and *his* eyes because he was the central character. Not until it was over should I have switched to Helen, presenting the next one from her point of view. I could then have shown her walking away down the street and, putting myself into her mind, revealed her compassion and her anxiety to help him without hurting his pride. Being alone, all this would be related through her thoughts and she would emerge as a more sympathetic character as a result.

First person singular

There is a common belief that writing in the first person singular is restrictive. I have heard teachers of creative writing, who should know better, issue it as a warning to new writers, discouraging them before they even try it.

'It's no use writing fiction in the first person because you can't reveal the thoughts and feelings of other characters that way. And you can't relate what's going on elsewhere because the "I" person can't possibly know. You can only convey all that in third person.'

From where did these misguided theories come? Who created this bogey to frighten an aspiring author who instinctively wants to write in first person singular and is now too afraid to try?

It certainly didn't come from the hundreds of successful authors, both past and present, who have used the first person for books that have won worldwide fame. The number is legion.

Take Charlotte Brontë's *Jane Eyre* for a start, a novel involving a host of characters whose actions, both on and off stage, are vital to the story's development. And how about Robert Louis Stevenson's *Kidnapped* and *Catriona*? Or Wilkie Collins's *The Woman in White*? What about *David Copperfield*? How did Dickens write *that* immortal tale? Nearer our own time, Daphe du Maurier showed us how to do it in those unforgettable novels, *Rebecca*, *My Cousin Rachel*, and *The Scapegoat*. Could the last one have been written in any other way, and could the first one have had a more haunting opening line than 'Last night I dreamt I went to Manderley again . . .'?

And did the readers of any of these books fail to sense or suspect the thoughts and feelings of other characters? In *Rebecca*, Max de Winter's turmoiled emotions, and the smouldering enmity of Mrs Danvers toward the very ordinary young woman who had replaced her late and beloved mistress, were conveyed strongly through the heroine's voice. Emotional tension, personal conflict, and individual reactions crackled from the pages.

And what about Hammond Innes's yarns, all written in the first person, teeming with varied characters and alive with action? Denis Bagley did it, too, and so have many, many others, but perhaps Susan Howatch has made the method distinctly her own.

For her, writing exclusively in the first person is obviously vital. Neither length nor time lapses daunt her. The 1,090 pages of *The Wheel of Fortune*, the panoramic sagas of *Penmarric* and *Cashelmara*, the lengthy pageantry of *Glittering Images*, all these and others of her books should be read and re-read by those who maintain that writing in the first person singular should be avoided.

In lighter vein, but confirming the effectiveness of the first-person approach, Mary Stewart's romantic suspense novels still retain the popularity they won in the 1950s, and for really brilliant first person writing read Thomas Hinde's *The Day The Call Came*. If you know the novel already you cannot fail to remember the important role of the narrator's wife, who never appears in the book but whose concern for her husband's sanity becomes increasingly evident until she brings about the climax of the story – but it is *he* who tells the tale.

As for conveying the secret thoughts and plans of other characters in a first person story, we have only to turn to Robert Louis Stevenson's *Kidnapped*. Remember David Balfour's arrival at the house called Shaws, to the surprise of old Ebenezer? From dialogue and character portrayal the reader guesses that the old man plans to get rid of the boy, but David doesn't have a suspicion until Ebenezer sends him up that unfinished staircase in total darkness. Not until the boy reaches the terrifying drop does he realise his danger, but readers sense it long before that.

As onlookers seeing most of the game we watch an unfolding drama, listen to every remark and every response and, if the book is well written, interpret them – as the 'I' person, who can see no side but his own, cannot. It is no different from real life, when other people know we are misunderstanding situations and wonder when we are going to wake up to the truth, or when a theatre audience watches a scene and, from dialogue and behaviour onstage, recognise what is going on in the minds of the characters and the meaning behind their remarks while the main participant in the play supposedly does not.

You can liken the situation to a triangle. Two people are in conversation with a third standing by, listening and watching. The first person misinterprets the second person's remarks and thereby creates a situation of misunderstanding and even enmity. The third person, the looker-on, listens to the same remarks and senses how wrongly the first person is interpreting them. Both central characters are unaware of the third person; only of themselves and the situation in which they are involved. So the looker-on can only listen and watch and wonder when the first person is going to wake up and how the situation is to be resolved.

The first person and the second are two points in the triangle and the third is you – the reader. The 'I' person may relate the story, but the onlooker always sees most of the game. That was how we accompanied David Balfour up those stairs at the instigation of old Ebenezer, and how we sensed that the old man was up to something.

Could that staircase scene in *Kidnapped* have been conveyed in third person? Undoubtedly, but would it have been so effective? We would have been *shown* the boy groping his way in the dark, but would not have climbed the stairs *with* him, sharing the experience *within his mind*. And in third person it would have been easy to switch to the old man's triumphant thoughts, giving the game away prematurely. Robert Louis Stevenson was plainly aware that, in this instance, first person singular imparted greater immediacy than third person would have done.

As for the question of how to convey, in first person treatment, the thoughts of two people when each is ignorant of the other's, turn to *Jane Eyre* and read that garden scene, with Mr Rochester pretending to be unaware of Jane's presence while she sits quietly sewing, eyes downcast, praying that he will not notice her but longing for him to do so. Told exclusively by her, we are not only aware of his approach but we guess why he is taking his time over it, pausing to examine a bush here, a flower there, never glancing toward her. We know exactly what is in his mind, while she is totally unaware of it. Read that scene and you will absorb the skill of first person writing and the dual emotions charging it.

A first person problem which does need to be mastered is that of conveying events which have taken place offstage; events the 'I' person has not witnessed but which must be revealed. It is all a question of communication. Remember that communication is a two-way thing; you receive it and you impart it. You talk to people and they talk to you. You listen, question, search, and you receive information, news, items of gossip. All this propels a first person story forward. And it must be natural, easy, flowing. . . .

'My dear, you should have been here when Mabel and John called! What *do* you think happened?'

Out pours the news, the picture takes shape, the narrator's mind does a U-turn and leaps ahead.

Or someone could burst into a scene, conveying news in a way which also tells us a lot about the speaker and just why she has arrived.

> The last person I expected to see, when I answered the door, was Brenda Forsythe. 'So glad you're in,' she said, strolling into the living room in that lazy way of hers. 'I missed you at Steve's house-warming last night. Did you forget, or something? Y'know, I thought you and he were just like *that*. . . .' She held up two fingers, close together. 'Anyway, it was a pity you missed it because who d'you think dropped in? Your dear Uncle James. It was as plain as a pikestaff why he was there – to drag his darling daughter away, your sweet little coz, Daphne. Oh yes, she was

there – wouldn't you have expected her to be? No, I thought perhaps you mightn't . . . anyway, there she was and having a whale of a time. I must say dear Papa showed admirable restraint. After downing a drink, he congratulated Steve on the way he's done the place up and said, "Get her back to the students' hostel by eleven, won't you?' and took his leave. We all fell about laughing then, because everyone knows – except you, perhaps? – that dear little Daph quit the hostel a week ago and moved in with Steve. . . . Perhaps that's why you didn't turn up, darling? Oh dear, have I said the wrong thing?'

I didn't answer. I couldn't. When she strolled to the front door I let her see herself out.

There is no need to say more in a scene like that. The 'I' person has said it all and you, the reader in the third corner of the triangle, know well enough what she is thinking and feeling *and* the malicious satisfaction of her visitor.

For a modern story there are many forms of communication, some of which are trite but nonetheless essential in our lives and therefore acceptable in fiction. There is the unpredictable telephone with its ability to ring at crucial moments; there is the news flash on TV or car radio; there is the unexpected letter that shocks or delights. All are perfectly legitimate forms of communication and can be used as advantageously in first person as in third.

Even the long arm of coincidence can, *if handled well*, be used convincingly from any viewpont but, unless it is unavoidable, try not to drag in the conveniently overheard conversation. The fact that in real life we overhear people talking in shops, buses, adjoining offices or elsewhere, does not make it easily acceptable in fiction. To have someone 'accidentally' hear a conversation (to which they then take time to listen from behind a half open door) smacks of dishonesty, like reading other people's letters. Your bad characters can do it. Your good ones can't.

Another first person singular problem which worries aspiring authors is how to depict the 'I' person's looks. They argue that you can't have a heroine boasting that she is pretty, or describing her features in detail. True. So you do it in other ways, as in the following extract from an early novel of mine:

Unlike myself, my mother had been a beauty, but she had passed on to me at least a measure of her looks, plus her tall slender figure. I had in my possession a miniature which my father always carried, painted when she was twenty, a year older than I am now. From it her large grey eyes, set beneath eyebrows that looked as if they had been stroked in by an artist's brush, conveyed humour and honesty and warmth. Her face was oval and her smooth hair was braided into a coronet. I had adopted this

style instinctively when the time came for me to put up my hair, and I
could well remember coming downstairs, standing before my father, and
seeing his start of surprise. Then his kindly eyes had filled with unexpected tears.

All he said was, 'You are so like her, it seems almost untrue. God has
been good to let her live again in you.'

(From: *The Arrogant Duke*.)

The passage conveys more than the heroine's appearance. It reveals
the love her parents had shared, her father's pride in his daughter, and
the girl's modesty ('Unlike myself, my mother had been a beauty').

In any genre and in any approach useful information can be conveyed indirectly. The fact that she had reached the age 'to put up her
hair' conveniently indicated that the story was a period one.

Mirrors are unfailingly useful, whatever the gender and whatever the
viewpoint, but particularly so in first person singular. Being an essential
part of our lives it doesn't smack of conceit when characters catch sight
of themselves and react accordingly. A Regency dandy can inspect the
tying of his high cravat and, in his thoughts, express his dissatisfaction
and his resolve to reprimand his manservant, thereby revealing both his
vanity and his pettiness. An aging woman can catch a glimpse and
mentally sigh for the days of her youth. 'Thank God he can't see me
now! I want him to remember me as I was.' And a modern young
woman can give voice to her reaction in this way:

Heavens, what a mess I looked, with my red hair scraped back to keep it
out of my eyes, smudges on my face, soil on my jeans, not even a comb
handy for a quick repair job and chunky clothes making me look more
tubby than ever! The reflection was thrown back at me from the green-
house windows as he came striding along the path, saying he'd been
ringing the front door bell without success so had come round the side to
look for me. Why are other women never caught at their worst? Why
couldn't *I* have been born a natural beauty who looks lovely even without
make-up?

There is more than just a woman's appearance there. There is
consternation because she has been caught at a bad moment by a man
whose reactions are obviously important to her. First person viewpoint
can convey vital touches as effortlessly as any other.

And, again from any viewpoint but of particular use in first person,
critical relatives can draw attention to a person's looks. A proud mother
can remark on her daughter's loveliness when dressed for a party, or
comment adversely on her make-up or on such things as artificual
highlights which, in her opinion, mar the girl's chestnut hair. A father

can growl his disapproval of a son's way-out gear, his terse comments painting an immediate vignette. Similarly, the briefest remarks can indicate an underlying attitude or emotion.

How, for instance, would you make a man reveal against his will, to a woman who angers him, that underneath it all she attracts him? Mary Stewart did it in *Madam, Will You Talk?* The heroine is kidnapping a child with the father in hot pursuit. (She has the wrong ideas about his motives, of course, but we have not because he is obviously the hero.) At length he catches up with her and, in a towering rage, he blazes, 'You beautiful bitch!'

Leave out the 'beautiful' and you have a man who hates her. Put it in and it reveals how he really sees her despite his anger and frustration, but because *she* is hating *him* she doesn't heed the adjective. Only to the reader does it speak volumes.

First person detached

When writing from this viewpoint, the narrator does not necessarily have to be the central character. This is especially useful when observing and commenting on them. If you feel you can tell the story more effectively through the mind of someone else, such as a son disclosing his father's story and the scandal or political drama that made him famous; or a mother telling the story of her daughter's rise to fame and fortune; or a sister revealing the reverse side of a picture hitherto accepted by everyone, then you will have the advantage of ready accessibility to scenes both on and off stage; a bird's eye view of all situations and events.

This can best be described as an extension of the first person viewpoint. It is popular in historical fiction, enabling the author to use an imaginary character – a servant, steward, or lady's maid – to relate a fictionalized version of events in contrast with recorded history; a sort of eye-witness account which would have been unheeded had such a lowly witness actually lived.

But remember that when using the voice of an onlooker, skilful writing is required to steer the reader's self-identification to the right quarter and to keep it there throughout the novel. One of the best examples of this approach is Bamber Gascoigne's *The Heyday*. In this novel a young man tells the story of his Edwardian grandmother in the brilliance of her theatrical prime. He never knew her. She has long been dead, but she is the central character throughout, not merely as an undying legend but as a living, breathing, vital person brought alive by the 'I' voice of her unknown grandson. Read it, enjoy it, and learn.

Now try it yourself

As a triple exercise, take the long-lost Elspeth Marshall from Chapter 3 and visualise her return to her native village. Decide at which point you will start; with her actual arrival, with the meeting of mother and daughter, or with a confrontation between Elspeth and the currently official Mrs Marshall at The White Horse. Then write the scene (a) in third person, (b) in first person, and (c) in first person detached (for which you will have to find the voice of an onlooker – a further exercise for your imagination).

When you have written all three, you will know in which viewpoint you feel most at ease. It will be the one you are anxious to continue writing.

When you have done so, try writing it from other angles. It will be good practice, and comparing the different results will not only be interesting but will demonstrate the effectiveness, or otherwise, of each approach. It will also confirm which is the right one for *you*.

8
Construction

Working to a blue print – or not?

A frequent question, from aspiring authors to published ones, is whether they write in longhand or onto a typewriter, to which, of course, 'word processor' has now been added.

My own answer is always the same: It doesn't matter which way you work, so long as you get the words down on paper. I have always used a keyboard, not only because my editorial experience taught me to but because, if writing at speed (or even otherwise), my handwriting becomes illegible and the mass of deletions, additions, and revisions I insert as I go along reduces the whole thing to a mess. The word processor, with its facility for correcting on screen, must have been designed for writers like me.

Invariably, the next question is: 'Do you work to an outline, or straight out of your head?'

Now we are on trickier ground. If I confess that I write 'straight out of my head' (which I do once I have a strong awareness of my 'lead' character and sometimes of supporting ones, and perhaps one or two possible situations, or simply an opening that I absolutely must get down on paper) there is the danger that new writers will assume it to be the correct way to work and that they are not being truly creative unless they do the same, so again my answer must be 'the choice is yours', but with certain qualifications.

If you have a writing tutor who advises you to work to a detailed synopsis, stay with it so long as you work confidently and happily that way, but when you are alone with your pen and your pile of blank paper don't be afraid to try another method if you feel the urge to.

If you find sticking to an outline difficult, or that you wander away from it as your story grows, don't worry – both can be very good signs indeed, indicating that your imagination is working well, that it is even taking control. This is commonly regarded as working by inspiration, but it is really your unconscious mind playing its part, as with my 'inspired' picture of the Edwardian mother and daughter who ultimately led me into *Dragonmede*.

We have already established that the unconscious mind is a store-house of facts and fancies, of forgotten experiences and impressions and thoughts and questions, all of which start surfacing when the conscious mind takes a rest. When these moments of inspiration come, seize them and store them, as I stored that mother and daughter. As your storehouse grows, jot down notes as memory-joggers. From these notes you can create an outline, building up a detailed plot if you feel you can work better that way.

Whether you decide to produce a blue print or not, you will be in good company. The late John Braine once told me that he always made a chapter by chapter outline and that Arnold Bennett did the same. The fact that I do not, I used to regard as a personal idioscyncracy and was relieved to learn that many professional authors work as I do, including Stan Barstow who, in a press interview, admitted that he is content to start from scratch, that with only the vaguest ideas he is prepared to write a couple of sentences and follow a thread which, months later, will 'lead him out at the end of the novel' but, in contrast, the French crime write, Georges Simenon, never started a novel without first drawing up a carefully detailed blue print.

Another crime novelist, Celia Fremlin, admits that she does the same, and while it seems reasonable that the intricacies of crime fiction should demand this method more than would a wholly emotional story, another popular crime writer, Marion Babson, shuns it. With only certain incidents and the crime's solution in mind she starts from scratch, telling herself the story as she goes along, as I do. She confesses that she would find less enjoyment in it otherwise.

Similarly, Harold Robbins, whose skilful plots are acknowledged worldwide, even by those who don't care for his books, does not work to a prepared plot. Few people believed this until his publisher, visiting him one day, saw a sheet of paper in his typewriter, stooped to read what was on it, found it exciting and promptly asked what was to happen next. 'I don't know,' said Robbins. 'My typewriter has broken down.'

It was the publisher, not Robbins, who vouched for this story and I relate it only to demonstrate that every author will eventually find his or her own method of writing, usual by a process of trial and error. Individuality being the very nature of authorship, it stands to reason that no hard and fast rules regarding working methods can be laid down. However, guidance *can* be offered to aspiring authors (such as my earlier advice on the construction of character dossiers). So can advice on overcoming certain technical difficulties and on the presentation of typescripts and the marketing of work (the latter two are featured in Chapter 11), but on how to decide on your approach to work you and you alone must be the final arbiter.

You may draw up dozens of plot outlines, only to find that when you get down to work your imagination takes control and you forget or ignore the lot of them. Words either spring into your mind and take you with them, or you stare at a blank sheet of paper and then reach thankfully for your blueprint. Either way can prove to be the best for *you*.

What I want to do is to free you from restriction, from any rigid ideas regarding the 'right' and the 'wrong' way to work. Most text books on the craft of writing advocate the use of a plot outline, sometimes to the extent of turning it into a laborious job guaranteed to quench an aspiring author's enthusiasm long before he even thinks of an opening line. One American text book even devotes the bulk to what the author apparently considers to be an infallible method of plot building, a complex exercise to be completed before a word of the novel is put down on paper.

The method consists of taking a large ringed looseleaf book and dividing it into manifold sections, each marked with gummed tabs. 'Calendar' is the first section, followed by another labelled 'Timing'; the first, for noting the dates on which work is carried out, and the second for recording the number of hours devoted to it (all of which could be jotted down in one's diary anyway). Yet more sub-divisions must be headed 'Plotting Begun' and 'Plotting Finished'; 'Estimated Length'; 'Chapters'; 'Chapter Pages' (with sample calculations such as '20 chapters, 15 pages each = 300 pages', disregarding the necessity for chapters to end only at a climactic or suspenseful moment, which alone dictates their length).

And that is not all, Still more sections should be labelled 'Situations'; 'Development of Situations'; 'Outcome of Developments'; 'Chronology'; 'Titles'; 'Theme'; 'Plotting'; 'Plotting Twists'; 'Characters'; 'Character Types'; 'Character Names'; 'Character Reactions'; 'Character Situations', and so on, all designed to force a beginner's mind onto complicated tramlines.

I decided to put it to the test. Taking a plot from one of my own published books, I dissected it according to the specifications, only to find, as I expected, that filling a large, thick record book with innumerable divisions devoted to so many specific headings resulted in a lot of unnecessary duplication – for example, 'Situations', 'Development of Situations', and 'Outcome of Developments', being inter-related to the point of being indivisible, therefore had to be slotted into all relevant sections and the same applied to almost every other aspect.

As a way of devising a complex Chinese puzzle I can think of no better method. So here let me sound a warning: don't bog yourself down with too much theorising. Don't place reliance on clever tricks.

Ignore advertisements for ready made plots 'Guaranteed to Sell Your Stories' (they won't) or to others guaranteeing to lead you to bestseller-dom overnight (they won't either).

And don't create a convoluted Spaghetti Junction of any outline you make. Keep it to essentials. You may find it quite sufficient to jot down reminders of forthcoming crises in the story as you currently visualise them, despite the likelihood of these events yielding to others as the book progresses. If you wish, and if you feel it keeps a goal in sight, you can also plan the end, but don't be surprised if that also changes long before you reach it. Constant change and unexpected developments are aspects of fiction writing that make it surprising and challenging and enjoyable, so don't worry if your blue print isn't strictly adhered to. How often have you veered away from a road map *en route* to a destination, and found it to be a better route than the one you planned?

Releasing the creative process

It is an undoubted fact that it is only when one is actually writing that one becomes truly creative. You may embark on a novel with only a minimal idea in your head, or perhaps an opening paragraph, or a scene which you think will come somewhere in midstream, or a beginning which you know will lead you somewhere, or an ending which shines like a light at the end of the tunnel. You may anticipate no problems at all from a carefully worked out plot, but the fact remains that at whatever stage you start to write, your story will only come to life once you start putting words down on paper. That is when creativity takes over and the real work begins.

The hours you devote to writing must depend on your personal circumstances; whether you have household or family responsibilities, or a daily job which you cannot afford to give up until you become well established as an author (and even then it is not always wise to). Whatever your situation, you must adapt your writing time to the demands of your lifestyle, but one thing I do advise – make a point of writing something every day, at whatever moment you can squeeze it in, whether in the train on your way to and from work, or for an hour when the children are at school, or during the evening while the family watches television. If you can fit in this session at the same time every day, so much the better. It will then become a habit as necessary to you as breathing.

I cannot emphasize strongly enough the value of a daily writing stint, even if it bears no relation to a story in its embryonic state. Write *any*thing and you will find that even when you think you are tired or uninspired, words will come and sentences will form and fatigue will slowly yield to creativity. Simultaneously, you will establish the habit of self-discipline, vital to every author.

But when finally sitting down to write that fictional work you have long been mulling over, you will find that you come face to face with certain structural problems, all of which have to be tackled and which all writers have to master. Let's take them one by one.

The narrative hook

In case you are unfamiliar with the term, it is used to describe an opening sentence, paragraph, or scene designed to grab the reader's attention and to provoke his curiosity to such a degree that he is compelled to read on.

Such a hook is desirable, even essential, at the start of a story. It can be startling, shocking, frightening, amusing or simply intriguing and, for preference, it should also convey some interesting or provocative information about the central character or characters, as a sort of appetiser whetting the reader's desire to learn more about them.

A fine example is the opening to Susan Howatch's novel, *The Rich Are Different*:

> I was in London when I first heard of Dinah Slade. She was broke and looking for a millionaire while I was rich and looking for a mistress. From the start we were deeply compatible.

Apart from the concise wit and the intriguing situation presented in those economical lines, they also convey some vivid character portrayal. We know, immediately, that he is ruthless as well as rich, selfish as well as shrewd; a man wanting to buy a mistress either because he shirks the responsibility of a wife or because he has one already, and his shrewdness prompts his quick assessment of Dinah Slade. Through his succinct observation we see the cold calculation of her and, because of it, we know she will be well able to hold her own. So there they are, the pair of them, ready to use each other without scruple. Compatible? Only as far as characteristics go and, for that reason, plainly in line for a head-on clash.

As readers, we find such a clever narrative hook intriguing. How will two such people make out? What happens next? We can't wait to discover.

For a chilling and challenging narrative hook to a chilling and disturbing story, let's take the opening to Dean Koontz's *Strangers*:

> Dominick Corvaisis went to sleep under a light wool blanket and a crisp

white sheet, sprawled alone in his bed, but he woke elsewhere – in the darkness of a large foyer closet, behind concealing coats and jackets. He was curled in the foetal position. His hands were squeezed into tight fists. The muscles in his neck and arms ached from a bad though unremembered dream.

He could not recall leaving the comfort of his mattress during the night, but he was not surprised to find that he had travelled in the dark hours. It had happened on two other occasions, and recently.

Where is he? How did he get into that clothes cupboard? Why the foetal position and the clenched hands? How did he travel in the dark hours without being aware of it? Our curiosity is whetted because this, obviously, is no ordinary case of sleep-walking. A shiver of expectancy is immediately stirred, impossible to resist.

In contrast, Thomas Hinde's opening to *Agent*, described in the press as 'a thriller-plus' and 'a bleak allegorical nightmare' – and acknowledged, nonetheless, as brilliant – grips the reader in an entirely different way. Here is the opening:

Lena is coming tonight.

She does mimes for me. Right in the middle of one she'll burst into tears, though she won't show it. She'll keep her face turned away from me, trying to hide them, continuing her act, but I'll catch glimpses of her crumpled face and see flashes of light reflected in the drops on it. Things have happened to Lena which should never have happened to a girl of her age – what a mistaken thought. It's because of what's happened to her that I so admire her.

What things have happened to her? What experiences are hidden behind her brave front? Who is she? And why does she come to this man (you know instinctively that the narrator is male) to do mimes for him, and at night? A narrative hook like that is irresistible because Lena is irresistible.

I said earlier that the narrative hook could also be amusing and provócative. That such an opening could seize a reader's immediate interest was proved as long ago as 1796 when Jane Austin began to write *Pride and Prejudice*:

It is a truth universally acknowledged, that a single man in possession of a good fortune must be in want of a wife.

It needs no more than that witty observation to plunge the reader into the fluttering excitement of ambitious Mamas and the coquettish rivalry of their daughters; no more than that to entertain and intrigue. Readers have been caught by that opening paragraph since it first appeared in print in 1813, and continue to be.

Four differing narrative hooks, and all successful.

A splendid and rewarding exercise, which can serve the dual purpose of stimulating your imagination and sparking further ideas for stories as well as training you in the art of writing good narrative hooks, is to write as many challenging beginnings as you can think of. Let them come out of the top of your head, giving no thought to tying them up with any story you may currently have in mind; in fact, the less they are associated with any specific piece of work is highly desirable at this stage. You are doing this exercise for the combined purposes of mastering the narrative hook and of jerking your unconscious mind into action. Out of the medley you produce, at least *one* hook is likely to seize your imagination, spurring you into creativity and a resultant story.

The chapter hook

This applies to chapter endings, when the curtain must descend at a point so dramatic or thought-provoking that readers are compelled to read on. This does not mean that every chapter break must be sensational or violent or melodramatic; it can finish on a note of quiet emotional conflict, or on one of question or doubt, but suspense of some kind *must* be maintained to whet the reader's interest.

The technique is identical to that used in drama. The curtain must descend at a point where the audience will be agog for it to rise again, so again I recommend that you read as many successful plays as possible. You will then recognise the value of surprise or shock or fear or bewilderment followed by the 'quick-cut', to be followed by more until the final curtain descends with all the questions answered and all loose ends tidied off, leaving the audience satisfied or justifiably *dis*satisfied if the ending is disappointing and flat. This same technique applies to storytelling. The reader's curiosity must be held until the close of the final chapter; if not, you have failed as a storyteller.

Chapter lengths

While on the subject of chapters, I must dispel a belief which is surprisingly prevalent among new writers, that chapters should be divided numerically, i.e., fifteen pages per chapter, or some similar number, no more and no less. I even saw a letter on the readers' page of a writers' magazine, written by an excited and self-congratulatory beginner, describing how she had 'hit on an excellent method of chapter-control' by dividing her sheaf of typing paper into batches of fifteen sheets, so that when she reached the end of the last one she knew she had completed another chapter. 'In that way,' she continued gleefully, 'you don't have to wonder when to end a chapter!'

I wanted to advise her to study more published novels; she would then have learned that length does *not* control chapter curtains, that they must rise and fall only when the right hooks are presented, no matter how long or how short the chapter may be as a result, otherwise not only the chapter but indeed the whole story will fall flat.

Transitions

One of the more worrying problems to new writers, and one of the easiest to handle, is the transition; how to bridge gaps in time, how to transport characters from place to place or from scene to scene. Such situations are unavoidable; they will recur regularly in any story.

Bear in mind that transitions serve two useful functions; they help to keep the action moving and they increase readability by contributing to a smooth and flowing style.

Let's write a bad transition and then analyse just why it is bad. We'll go to Chapter 6 and Ruth's visit to her friend Sylvia:

> Once she had made up her mind, Ruth decided to call on Sylvia without delay. Opening the hall cupboard, she seized her coat blindly, shrugged into it and set out to walk, thinking that to do so, rather than to drive, would help to calm her down. Today, however, the distance seemed longer than usual because she was impatient to get there, impatient to seek her friends' reassurance and help. Along Heathfield Road she walked, turned right into the seemingly endless stretch of Mulberry Lane, and began to wish that she had driven after all. At last she reached the turning where Sylvia lived, but as she approached the house apprehension seized her. What if she were making a mistake? What if both Sylvia and Peter refused to believe her?
>
> Momentarily, she faltered, then resolutely walked on. With the same resolute step she approached their front door and rang the bell. Even then she was tempted to turn back, but the door was opened immediately and Sylvia stood there.
>
> 'Ruth, how nice to see you! Come along in. I was thinking of you only today . . .'

The meeting could then follow as written, but its impact would be weak. Such a clumsy and lengthy transition holds up the action because it adds nothing. There is no necessity to follow a character from place to place, or to describe in detail how they get there, unless something happens *en route* which affects the story.

Compare the foregoing with the following:

> Once she had made up her mind, Ruth called on Sylvia without delay. She was glad when her friend promptly answered the door because it gave her no time to hesitate or withdraw. (The scene then proceeds as written.)

Scene should immediately follow scene without any surplus prose acting as a brake between them. And remember that your readers don't want or need to be led by the hand. If it is written well, they can grasp a situation and visualise a scene without unnecessary elaboration. Retard the action with trivial details and excess wordage and their interest, like the story, will flag.

Another effective way of handling a transition is to insert a gap in the narrative. This is commonly called a 'space break' and is particularly useful in indicating time switches. In Ruth's case we could use it in the following way, changing her method of approach:

> To make sure that Sylvia would be in, Ruth telephoned her.
> 'May I pop round to see you?' she asked. 'I'd like to talk . . .'
> 'My dear, I'd be delighted. Come at once – we haven't had a good natter for ages!'
>
> Ten minutes later, Ruth was ringing the doorbell . . . (and the scene continues as before).

See how simple it is to handle transitions? There is no need to be afraid of them or to try to dodge them. Make them serve you as effectively as they are designed to, and they will cease to be bogies.

The flashback

As a reader, I find nothing more 'off-putting' than slices of retrospection if they are badly handled. Flashbacks are often useful, sometimes essential, but very often used as a means of escape from a situation which is proving difficult to handle. To indulge in the brief reminiscent thoughts of a character offers a convenient way out while seeking a solution to a problem, but the reader may well feel frustrated if, at a moment when he was expecting the story to move forward, he finds it going backward, and if this is indulged in too often, without advancing the tale, he will put the book aside and not pick it up again.

When that happens, the flashback has indeed been badly handled. It should never be a 'marking time', never a hold-up in any shape or form. Like everything else in the writing of popular fiction, the flashback should help to advance the story, never to retard it. That is why it is so difficult to use. Marching backward never advances anyone's footsteps, but they *can* retrace a few steps in order to take a detour which will bring them out at a point further ahead. That is what the well handled flashback does.

When writing my trilogy of novels about the Drayton family, I was faced with the enormous problem of bridging gaps between the generations without repeating large slices of information with which earlier readers would already be acquainted. (I will touch on this in more detail in Chapter 10, on the writing of sequels). It was essential, in developing the character of the last-born son, to reveal resemblances to his dead father *and* to the circumstances of his father's death although it happened before the son was born.

Since the past influenced the present, certain revelations had to be made. To actually re-live them retrospectively meant jumping back into the previous book, with consequent repetition and no advancement in the sequel, so the obvious method was to filter hints through the medium of the son's thoughts when he occasionally recalled veiled references to his father's death, through his consequent curiosity, and through the conversation of other characters when, observing his behaviour, they remarked on his resemblance to his father and recollected certain past episodes. This method served the purpose of awakening the reader's interest in the past, throwing light on unanswered questions and provoking more, and arousing curiosity about the present.

That is the value of the flashback, providing it is well used. It can also be valuable in depicting nostalgia, such as a woman's longing for a vital moment in her past, or a turning point in her life which is suddenly recalled by a vivid reminder of some kind – such as a musical strain, or a perfume. To me, one of the most evocative scents, which seems sadly lost today, is that of mignonette, once used as a cottage border plant. It was a modest flower, sometimes regarded as a weed and possibly, for that reason, falling from favour, but I believe that at the time of the Civil War it was widely cultivated. It was therefore useful in inspiring a flashback about a young woman whose village lover was away fighting for the Roundheads. Dutifully tending her mother's garden one evening, the perfume of mignonette revived in her memory the moment when he had proposed to her and the necessity for secrecy because her mother would have opposed such a marriage. The flashback served the purpose far better than a trite recitation of facts, lacking in nostalgia or emotional depth.

To make the most of the short flashback it is important to keep it well confined – commonly known as 'framing'. This means restricting it (as with the girl thinking of her lover) within the immediate moment and, at the end of the flashback, reverting to that moment. In other words, you don't leave the scene at all: you don't jump back in time *and in action* and then jump back to the present. Of course, it can be (and has been) done, but to be really effective you merge the two so that there is no stalling, no deliberate halt. That is why a few short flashbacks are often more effective than several long ones from which the reader has to be jolted back to the main body of the story.

Even so, I don't recommend the use of too many short flashbacks or they can appear as jagged interruptions. Use them sparingly and well, as naturally as thought, and they will merge into the story's context effortlessly.

Now, of course, you are recalling published novels which have depended largely on lengthy flashbacks, and others which have begun in the present and have then continued retrospectively throughout the book, returning to the present only at the end. And you are justified in doing so. Skilled authors have produced successful novels that way, but I don't recommend that beginners should try to until they have had some experience. Whole chapters in flashback can lead to confusion until you have mastered the technique of getting back onto the main road again.

One last word on this retrospective device – write in the pluperfect tense as little as possible. This is sometimes called 'the had-had syndrome' (he had had, she had had, they had thought, had said, had gone, had done . . .). To read a whole passage written in this way can be jerky and irritating so, to avoid that, merely start the retrospective piece in the pluperfect, using it perhaps once or twice at the beginning, but from then on continue in the normal tense until the end, when you can use it again to indicate that the flashback is over. This will ease you back into the scene without any jerking or jarring and maintain the smooth flow of your writing.

Clichés

Just as the use of too many adverbs, adjectives, and dialogue tags betray an inexperienced writer, so does the cliché betray the lazy one. To describe someone as 'lively as a cricket', 'proud as a peacock', 'mad as a March hare', or 'poor as a church mouse' (or any other hackneyed phrase) indicates that the writer can't be bothered to think of anything more original. This kind of writer will also use the cliché opening (e.g., 'The moon rode high in the sky . . .'; 'It was a dark and stormy night . . .') because he won't spare the time to exercise his imagination. The cliché is a dangerous short cut, a device which enables you to toss off a piece of writing with a minimum of thought.

But, being mortal, we are all in danger of falling into its trap. Nothing is so insidious as the cliché and nothing so effectively destroys stylish prose, so when you have finished a piece of work and are checking your final draft, wage war on it.

Endings

In many ways the winding up of your story is more difficult than the beginning, even though you may see it clearly ahead of you. At the start, you have the whole vast canvas spread before you, yours to fill in any way you wish; at the end it has shrunk to a minimum and you are faced with the final test. In this limited space you must present the closing sequence of events, the finale which readers are going to remember with enjoyment, if it is satisfying, or with disappointment if it is not. On it can hinge their choice of whether to read your next book, or not to bother.

Think of that, and you won't toss off a slap-dash finish just because you want to be rid of the whole thing and to put your feet up at last. Don't imagine that because three quarters or more of the book has been exciting and well written, a swift curtain at the end is all that's needed because only the body of the book will be remembered and that so long as everything is rounded off somehow, readers can have no cause for complaint. They can, and they will.

Apart from their disappointment, however, there will be your own when a publisher's reader describes the book as a let-down and doesn't recommend its publication or, if it does get that far, word spreads that it fizzles out at the end, and copies remain on the shelves of booksellers and libraries. After many months of hard work, that situation can be a bitter one, so it is up to you to avoid it. You can do so by taking a deep breath when you see the end looming ahead and giving it as much thought as you gave to the beginning. Plan to leave your readers with a feeling of satisfaction and enjoyment on a par with the anticipation and excitement you engendered at the start.

Whatever the pessimists might say, I firmly believe that readers prefer a happy ending to a miserable one. That doesn't mean that they don't want anything 'true to life'; it means that even the saddest of stories can at least finish on a note of hope. Not everyone 'enjoys a good cry'; certainly not the readers of popular novels whether they be mystery, suspense, historicals, or romance. As for crime novels, what the reader wants and expects and fully deserves to get is a surprising and convincing solution.

In short, the best ending is the one that totally satisfies. To achieve this take good care not to let the action flag. Speed up the pace toward the end, but on a note of sustained excitement. And don't let it drag on for a dozen or so pages after the climax has been reached. Wind up the whole thing speedily, then leave your readers at the peak, reluctant to come down to earth. Such an ending will leave them wanting to read another of your novels.

9
Beating the Block

Recognising the causes

I often wish the name 'writer's block' had never been thought of because it seems to plant a conviction, in the minds of beginners, that the condition is part and parcel of authorship, even that one cannot *be* an author without suffering the dreaded disease. This is as misleading as advertising propaganda designed to convince people that they need some new product to cure ailments they never knew they had.

That all writers get stuck at times is well known, but anything that exaggerates a condition to the point of creating alarm is undesirable. The sudden inability to put words on paper is every author's bogey, but to give it such a heavy-handed name as 'writer's block' makes it sound immovable, incurable, and final.

It isn't.

Early in Chapter 1, I mentioned two ways of dealing with two aspects of the problem; fear of starting ('starter's block') and the fear of being unable to follow up success ('the follow-up block'). I will now discuss others, with equally practical ways of coping.

The first step is to analyse what 'writer's block' is. George Eliot aptly summed it up as 'the pitiable instance of long incubation producing no chick'. There was no specific name for it in her day, but temporarily drying up was as familiar to authors then as it is now. Thomas Carlyle advised his poor wife, Jane, to abandon writing when the muse deserted her (as it frequently did after he became her husband), assuring her that 'eventually' the words would flow again, but this was suspect advice from a man who plainly did not want her to write at all, but only to be the dutiful wife catering for his needs and protecting him against disturbance.

So let's dismiss Thomas Carlyle, even though we cannot dismiss the block problem which can eventually convince an author that he has written himself out, but such a case is rare and to anticipate such a thing is pessimistic. There are ways in which to confront and reverse the problem, so that you will eventually say, 'I never suffer from writer's block'. No one will believe you, but that won't worry you because you will be happily writing again.

Fear is invariably the main root of the problem. Fear can be mentally paralyzing and, so long as you let it take over, the dreaded block will master you instead of *you* mastering *it*.

The first step is not only to acknowledge fear, but to diagnose the cause. There are numerous self-help books on the subject by so-called experts, all of which, like medical dictionaries, will bog you down with sometimes incomprehensible terms and a wealth of symptoms which will convince you that you suffer from the lot. I propose to discard these experts along with Thomas Carlyle.

My only qualification is that I have survived every occupational hazard, including writer's block, and in the process have identified the different types and the various causes. Let's take them one by one.

The outline block

This can be suffered by those who are convinced that a writer *must* produce an outline because without it he won't know where he is going. Having already touched on that, it is unnecessary for me to dwell on it here, except to add that if you *are* working to an outline and have reached a point where a carefully planned scene breaks down, leaving you convinced that all that talk about characters 'taking over' and a story 'taking off on it own' is a load of rubbish, there can be a very simple reason for this apparent disaster, and one which many a writer has shared. You may have chosen the wrong background, either social or physical, for your main character or characters, so see if you can switch it to another setting in which the behaviour you anticipated will be more natural.

Or, if you are writing an historical, check whether the time and place in which you have set your story (say seventeenth century London) has been researched thoroughly. It is important to remember, not only that it would be vastly different geographically from today, but culturally too. Check whether your blue print takes these changes fully into account, including changes in outlook and attitudes as well as in fashion, customs, and life styles. It is useless to expect your characters to react to specific situations in a specific way, if inappropriate to their generation or time. They will metaphorically thumb their noses at you and your carefully mapped plan will fall apart.

When that happens, you feel a failure, but you are not. Bear in mind that a block is simply a red flag of warning, a signal that you are on the wrong lines. It is giving you a chance to rethink and rewrite.

Appropriately, I touched on 'starter's block' in Chapter 1, also on the 'follow-up block' which sometimes comes in the wake of sudden success, so the ways of dealing with them need not be reiterated. We can now go on to:

The ambition block

Again, the name is my own for a condition which afflicts many aspiring authors, also many who have already achieved publication but feel dissatisfied without really knowing why. Unhappily, it can put a brake on a writer's career if he or she allows it to.

It is attributable to being too self-demanding, to setting your expectations too high, and to striving to emulate big literary names at whose shrines you have long worshipped. You read them with admiration and respect because they win awards and the highbrow literary journals praise them and that, you believe, is the only *real* success. You therefore aspire to the same heights, become frustrated, and dry up.

You have come up against the 'ambition block' head on, and it is experienced by many who won't admit that they used to read less scholarly writings with enjoyment, but of course put away such childish things when they set out to become serious (i.e. highbrow) writers. Not only would they not dream of reading at that level now, they wouldn't dream of writing down to it. It would be demeaning. So they struggle and flounder and finish up in the most dangerous state of all, totally blocked and convinced they will never succeed.

If you are one of these people, take stock of yourself. Force yourself to be honest – and don't write another word until you have spent six months reading those authors whom you think you should despise because they *sell*. You won't enjoy all of them, you may not even finish some, but make a note of those which leave you with a feeling of satisfaction and enjoyment and then acknowledge that you have been reading at a level in which you feel at home. Then confess why. Confess that they struck a sympathetic chord, reflecting your own need to write the same type of fiction with the same spontaneity and the same lack of self-consciousness.

In this way you will discover your natural bent. Recognising your limitations, *and being happy within them*, you will return to your pen or your keyboard with this particular block effectively vanquished. And you won't be a bad writer because you have been sensible enough to come to terms with the truth.

The vanity block

You can cure this easily if you want to. It comes from trying to adhere to a picture of 'how an author should work' and even of 'how an author should look' (i.e. dripping with mink, if female; driving around in the latest Mercedes, if male). The picture becomes lodged in your mind, you can *see* yourself in the role, and to achieve it you know you must emulate the working methods of those who have already done so.

You have read how one particularly successful author writes from nine to five daily, with half an hour's break for lunch, or another who works every morning, relaxes in the afternoon playing golf, and returns to another long creative stint from eight to midnight. So *that's* how it's done, you think (very impressed) and if you do the same you too will succeed! So your household and your family become geared to this routine and then down comes the block. You are unproductive, worried, depressed, familiar once more with a sense of failure.

Here you must be honest again. Face up to the fact that *you* are not *that* person. You are someone else; different; individual. In the silence inflicted by this particular block your ego is urging you not only to think again, but to adapt to the circumstances of your life and to follow your personal inclinations. It will cease to protest once you abandon the idea that you must follow someone else's pattern.

The criticism block

This is perhaps the hardest to beat. I first experienced it at the age of thirteen and I remember it well. I read aloud a story I had written, of which I was secretly proud. I therefore expected my family to be proud too. Instead, one sister called it daft, another soppy, and the third laughed her sides out. I fled in tears. Never again would I write. Never, *ever*.

A day or two later my English teacher asked why I had not submitted a class essay. When she heard the reason she was not unsympathetic, but warned that until I learned to accept criticism I would fail at whatever I undertook. She then gave me a week to produce my essay and added another piece of advice. 'Remember that those who mock are usually those who can't do what *you* can.'

This truth has helped me to survive, but it is hard to cling to when comments are scathing. If we were not sensitive we would not be writers, so we have to learn to live with this sensitivity and try to hide it. The hurts will linger, but you have to expurgate them; if you don't, they will block creativity more effectively than any other cause.

One good way to counter criticism is to retaliate in some brief and pertinent way (if you have the opportunity and can think of it quickly enough!). There is a story about a popular romantic novelist of the thirties, Ruby M. Ayres, a large and genial lady who was apparently a match for anyone. In a fashionable London bar one day a patronising woman drawled, 'My dear, I can *never* read books like yours!'

'Maybe not,' boomed Ruby, 'but can you write 'em?'

Once you are published, a good way to counter criticism is to look at your royalty figures. They can exhilarate you more than any praise because they would not be there if denigration of your work was universal.

You are sure to devise your own ways of beating the block, as I have. I used to suffer difficulty in re-launching after a break. I now resolutely leave a scene unfinished when (but only when) I can see precisely where it is going. I can then return to my desk quite ready to continue; no permanent break, no block.

Another method, and one which I recommend as a way of picking up the threads, is to go back several pages and to start editing. Rewriting or reshaping bad patches creates a launching pad and words then continue to flow when the next sheet of paper is a blank one.

Both are simple remedies, but don't forget that, whenever you get stuck, the first step is to root out the cause of the problem.

10
Sagas, Sequels, and Settings

The continuing tale

Every writer of fiction feels possessive toward his characters, but even stronger is the feeling of being possessed *by* them. Sometimes this lingers after a novel is finished, as if they were hammering on the door, demanding readmission. (Surely Mazo de la Roche was possessed by the Whiteoak family, and James Galsworthy by the Forsytes, and Hugh Walpole by the Herries?) Even so, I was surprised when the Drayton family 'took me over'. At the end of the first volume, *The Drayton Legacy*, I fully expected to say goodbye to them and to open my mind to others. I might have achieved this had the Draytons allowed me to, but they did not, and when my publishers suggested I should write a sequel I found, after initial resistance, that I wanted to, if only to get that 18th century family of potters out of my system.

Once acknowledging the truth, I also acknowledged that part of my reluctance had been due to apprehension. I had never tackled a sequel and had heard, from some who had, that it was a difficult process to be resolutely avoided. To me, that was a challenge, as a result of which I learned that writing a sequel is not the terrifying experience I expected. Evidence of this was supported by the many family sagas on library shelves and the number of authors who had woven entirely new stories about various branches of a family. Thus I realised that my sequel had to be a novel capable of standing on its own. Even though growing out of what had gone on before, it had to be a separate and self-contained book which could, if necessary, be read out of sequence although retaining relationship with its forerunner.

Ironically, the final decision to tackle it was spurred by a sequel written by an author who went about the task in entirely the wrong way. I read it with a combination of astonishment and not a little annoyance. I had not bought Book 2 expecting to find repetitive material from Book 1, but in the belief that the second book would be as new to me as the first. Instead, almost the first quarter of the sequel was re-hashed material from its predecessor, some paragraphs even being reprinted verbatim, with slices of new material injected here and there. Not until page 217 did this unsatisfactory sequel really begin to cover fresh fields.

I am not denying that it is necessary to acquaint new readers with essential facts from the past, but it should be done in a wholly new way so that the readers of the first book find it acceptable.

I learned other valuable lessons from this cut-the-corner author; that *Drayton 2* (*The Potter's Niece*) should not only contain *no* reprinted material, even in patches, but that slabs of retrospection should not be inserted just to put new readers in the picture (or to pad out the story); that the earlier part of Book 2 should not be a virtually condensed synopsis of what had gone before because people who had read Book 1 would be likely to remember a great deal and feel defrauded (as I did) if it were fed to them again; and, finally and most important, that unless I could come up with a totally new novel I should not attempt a sequel at all.

The Drayton Legacy was never intended to be the first of a series. It had been written as a single, complete book and a single, complete book it was; all problems solved, all questions answered; all loose ends tidied off. So what threads were left for me to pick up and weave into a sequel? That is the question you must ask yourself if you too consider writing a successor to a story.

My answer was – none.

It was the characters, not the situations on which the curtain had fallen, that cried out to live again. Some of the family had, of course, gone, but I could see how their deeds and misdeeds forecast the future. Such shadows and reflections, through their influence on events, would become a natural part of the sequel and take the story forward again. So, too, would Drayton descendants, some of whom had already been born.

So back I had to go to the family, whose ancestors had been itinerant potters since the fifteenth century, digging their clay wherever they found it and peddling their wares throughout the highways and byways of England until one enterprising Drayton set up the first family pottery in an abandoned barn. Such specific references could be omitted from Book 2 since they would not actually advance the story, but by putting them into the mouth of one of the older generation, talking about the family heritage to a younger one, I could see that they would add colour and interest while providing new readers with snippets of background information – snippets which earlier readers might well have forgotten and therefore welcome.

So I pass on to you something else I learned; sift your existing material carefully. Don't reject *all* interesting items from the past. Used judiciously they will highlight your story; newly told and newly minted they will not be rehashed material in any way at all.

But now to the first major problem.

Seeking an opening from the past

This did not appear to be a major one until I turned to the ending of *Legacy*. It had closed with the murder of the tyrannical Joseph whose wife, Agatha, pretended to mourn him while his sister, Phoebe, openly wept for him. Phoebe had idolized her brother and held him up as an example to her own errant husband. Consequently there had been rivalry between the two women and at the close of the book Phoebe had triumphed over her sister-in-law by being the first to become pregnant, inwardly crowing because Agatha, now widowed, would never be. It also meant that Phoebe's child would inherit vast estates.

Plainly, there had to be an unexpected start to the sequel and there it was, staring me in the face. What if Agatha had discovered, *after* her husband's funeral, that she too was pregnant, and what if she had later given birth to a son and Phoebe to a daughter? Their positions would be dramatically reversed.

But when to take the curtain up? If I did so at that point, the story threatened to meander through the son's uneventful childhood. With the object of pushing the action forward, a leap ahead was desirable, touching only briefly on the child's formative years. Sojourns into childhood memories were therefore permissible, usefully demonstrating the theory of 'the child is father to the man' and thus indicating his potential character. They could raise questions and whet the reader's curiosity. They could also serve as bridges, linking the past with the present. Such treatment would not only cater for the new reader, but satisfy earlier ones who, after a lapse of time, might appreciate a small memory jog.

In short, I had to keep in mind those who had read the first book and those who had not. Both had to be catered for and I soon realised that satisfying one while satisfying the other was perhaps the trickiest part of all. And I realised something else: that when writing a sequel or a trilogy (into which I developed the Drayton family, finishing with *The Rival Potters*) the author has to look continuously toward the future while continuously being aware of the past, but must never step actively back into that past. Its tentacles must only reach out when needed to propel the sequel forward or to shed light on a current situation.

When you, the aspiring author, are faced with a sequel, you will find conversation a good, succinct, and useful way in which to present necessary facts about the past – through one character telling another about it, or through two or three characters exchanging reminiscences, or even through the desire of one person to clarify or atone for past misunderstandings – but always and only if such reminiscence or clarification is essential in advancing the new story. And briefly. Brevity can not only have a greater impact, but it forestalls hold-ups. The book must surge forward at the same pace as its predecessor, with the same independence of structure and plot.

Bearing these lessons in mind, you will find that, once launched, your sequel will proceed at the same tempo and with the same amount of effort required for any novel and that it is therefore no easier nor more difficult to write. And if you put your heart into it, it will be as alive to your readers as the first book, establishing itself in their minds so that, at the end, they are wanting yet another to follow, and when you are faced with that, you will be faced with the all-important matter of updating your background.

Nothing in life remains static, which means that backgrounds, and the people you set down in them, will change from period to period. Between the action in Books 1 and 2 of my saga was a gap of twenty-one years; between Books 2 and 3, another fifteen. In those time-gaps not only fashions had changed, but industrial methods and, to a certain degree (but not so greatly as in a modern story) lifestyles and attitudes, all of which had an influence on situations, on developments, and on characters. Inevitably, this meant further research and that brings us to a very necessary discussion of that important subject.

Getting the background right

There seems to be a widely held belief, among new writers, that background is simply the geographical setting of a story, but it is a great deal more than that. It is not only the place where your characters live and work, but how they live and the work they do; it is their cultural level and the strata of society to which they belong; it is customs, habits, traditions, language, food, dress, beliefs and attitudes. It can be city or country life, moral or immoral, ethnic or non-ethnic, industrial or leisured, rich or poor. Above all, background is made up of the essential details that give authenticity to your story, whatever its time and setting.

The suggestions I give for getting your background right are the result of experience over many years. Don't be put off by the fact that I sometimes issue them as warnings. 'How not to' can often be more constructive than 'how to'; 'don't' more effective than 'do'.

Don't fake background details. Don't imagine that readers won't be knowledgeable enough to catch you out, or that if you choose an unusual subject and 'blind them with science' a few fabrications will pass unnoticed. The fact that your subject is unusual will be no guarantee that amongst the mass of readers there won't be one, and possibly more, who will actually be well versed in it and will spot at least one mistake – and one is one too many.

No author can afford to lose credibility. If your main character breeds huskies in Alaska or rare Chinese pheasants in Kiang-si, don't think you can get away with imagining the creatures' eating habits or any other detail about their rearing. Learn everything there is to learn about rearing huskies or Chinese pheasants or you can take a level bet that someone, somewhere, will know and will enjoy putting you right.

The easiest way to safeguard against error is, of course, to write only about things you know, but sometimes that can be restrictive and, if you have a fertile and questing imagination, it will be carrying you into realms that need exploring. That is where research comes in.

Research

When I began writing this book I made up my mind that I would *not* quote the much-used cliché about the iceberg – that only the tip shows, but beneath lies the unseen mass without which it would sink – yet now that I need an example of the amount of research necessary to add authenticity to a background, I can think of none better. Only a small amount of your researched material may, and probably will, be needed to give conviction to your story, but that small amount must be supported by a depth of knowledge. When an author writes with authority, it shows. When he merely slots in scraps of information picked up here and there, it also shows. And when that happens credibility flies out of the window.

Perhaps you have decided to set your story in Singapore or some other distant place. It would help enormously if you could spend some time there, but if this is not possible you do the next best thing; you read about the place, browse through travel brochures, hire video films and dream up your own imaginary picture with the result that what you eventually write reads like a travelogue. That is *not* your aim and you vow never again to write about places you don't actually know. Is this the right decision? No.

Many highly successful books have been set in countries physically unknown to their authors, but the research which produced them has been extensive and intensive. It has gone 'way beyond the travel brochure stage. It has delved into the country's history; it has studied the inhabitants' way of life, their culture, architecture, educational system, religion, traditions, and every other possible aspect. All this, and more, has provided that great mass of material which gave strength and support to the essential amount threaded into the story, elevating it above superficiality.

If, however, your story is set almost exclusively in the industrial or manufacturing scene, you will need less of the social scene outside it. Concentrate on the business background with its competitiveness, its wheeling and dealing, its personal relationships and animosities and jealousies, and the manifold aspects of its self-enclosed world. You can inter-relate the stories of a dozen characters within it without any need for stepping outside (read Arthur Hailey's *Hotel* and *Airport* as examples) but the need for accuracy is as great and every detail must count. It is penetrating research on this scale that has produced many successful blockbusters.

Take heart, there is no need to exhaust yourself in the process. You don't have to carry out *all* your research in one massive effort, unless you feel you would work better that way. Some authors do, but many hard working writers do as much preliminary work as is needful to get started and continue as they write, halting when coming to a part which needs strengthening with additional information or which presents specific problems. The experience is rather like coming up against a road block, forcing you to halt until the way is clear – except that you have to clear it yourself.

These breaks can often act as a stimulus, forcing you away from your desk to enjoyable sessions in your local reference library, or forays into bookshops, including second-hand ones which frequently yield treasure-trove. You will certainly want and *need* to build up your own reference shelves at home, not only to save time but for the satisfaction of having essential books (including those you enjoy browsing in) ready to hand.

You will also seek interviews with experts. A best-selling American author uses this method for almost his entire research, going to people at the top and at every strata downward until he has notebooks crammed with information covering every level of the enterprise, and then asking for more if necessary. It is rarely, if ever, refused.

You will find that people love to talk about the sphere in which they work, and especially about their particular participation in it, but you would be wise to consult more than one because on some points experts in most areas will disagree. It will be up to you to assess their opinions and decide which to accept. On debatable points, try to get written confirmation of their statements so that you may quote them should you be challenged. It would also be fair to ask the experts for permission to do so if necessary. If they prefer not to be quoted, you have good reason to doubt their reliability. If they agree without hesitation, you can be confident that their information is sound.

What other sources will you consult, apart from major libraries? There are public record offices, museums, local and church archives, private memoirs if you can gain access to them, and countless other sources, all of which are listed in Ann Hoffman's *Research For Writers*. This valuable book should be one of the first you buy for your personal reference library, for it not only lists extensive research sources, but gives expert advice on research methods and on some of the pitfalls to be avoided by the inexperienced writer.

Using your research effectively

When you have assembled your background material, don't feed it into your story in huge chunks. Spread it unobtrusively so that atmosphere is built up imperceptibly and naturally. Never stop your story dead in its tracks for long passages of description or information. Always remember that readers can't be conned. They recognise when an author is cramming in material just for the sake of doing so, and they will put their own interpretation on it – usually that he is trying to impress them with his knowledge or, if the background is an exotic one, trying to show that he is accustomed to luxury travel. Their assumptions are, of course, wide of the mark, but how are they to know that the author just can't bear to waste a scrap of his precious research?

All the same, economy must be the keynote. Too much elaboration can burden a story, so don't overpaint the picture. I recently read a novel set in Burma, crammed with repetitive Burmese names and forms of address, lumbered with too much Burmese history and littered with incomprehensible Burmese words and titles. A glossary was inserted at the end of the book to aid interpretation, but continual resource to it meant breaks in concentration so that eventually one ceased to bother. It was the author's first novel so one made allowances; but not for the publisher, who should have known better.

Integrate your background facts with the action and the story will be a hundred times more real. Interweave such paragraphs with the execution of the plot, and your readers will not only be carried along with it, but absorb its atmosphere.

But what of all that wasted research? you may ask. What of all the precious material I didn't use, what am I supposed to do, throw it away?

Indeed no. Save it. You have a precious stock for future books; the mere fact that you have such a store will inspire you to write another. For years I hoarded information about Victorian womanhood from the time dear Mama launched her daughters onto the marriage market to the time they became wives and mothers. Social, marital, sexual, child care, domestic, fashion, transport, etiquette; every possible aspect of a woman's life whatever her standing, from the lowly coachman's wife in the mews to the high society hostess; from the sweat-shop seamstress to the middle and upper class housewife; from the 'fallen woman' to the well kept society mistress; from the kitchen maid to the house-keeper; from the country miss who never set foot in London to the debutante's presentation at Buckingham Palace. I amassed so much that even after four Victorian novels I had used scarcely half of it. Eventually I collected it all together and turned it into a comprehensive reference book, *The Model Wife, Nineteenth Century Style*. So never part with researched material. You never know what you can do with it.

The period novel v. the historical

It is not the intention of this book to concentrate on the writing of one particular genre; indeed, it is impossible since the term 'popular fiction' covers such a vast range. But while we are on the subject of research it seems apt to discuss one genre which can demand more research than any other; with the exception, perhaps, of a modern blockbuster concentrating on the complexities of a vast technological background. The genre I am referring to now is the historical and its close rival, the period novel.

Some people argue that they are one and the same thing, but to me they are not. The dividing line may be thin, but it is there, and to define it should be of some help.

An historical novel focuses on recorded historical events and, in particular, on the people associated with them; people who actually lived and whose names have passed into posterity, either because of their achievements, because of their birth, or because they just hap-pened to be around when some memorable event occurred, and involved them.

In contrast, for plot and characterization the period novel relies entirely on the author's imagination. This is not to say that the back-ground can be inaccurate. Far from it. As much research must go into the period novel as into the true historical. Authenticity of fashions, food, housing, transport, domesticity, speech, education (or lack of it), etiquette, manners and morals, social strata, family life, plus political background of the times – all must be researched and accurately presented in both types of fiction.

To differentiate, let's take the period novel. Even if politics don't play an active or influential part in it, passing references to the reigning monarch or prime minister, or the fact that a specific battle such as the Crimean or the American War of Independence is raging overseas, add authority and colour to the background and help to pinpoint the exact era, but that can be the extent of their usefulness if the author wishes.

Examples of true period novels are Georgette Heyer's Regency and Georgian romances, as opposed to her historical novels such as *The Infamous Army*, *Royal Escape*, and *The Conqueror*. It is for her imaginative and sparkling period pieces that she is most remembered and which won her the greatest acclaim.

Plainly, she loved the Regency and Georgian periods above all, her ear so attuned to speech modes of the time that she could create pseudo phrases and slang expressions which sounded as authentic as those that were. Her readers accepted these imaginary colloquialisms as genuine examples of Georgian and Regency speech. Many are untraceable through the usual idiomatic research channels, but it is easy to imagine that had Regency bucks and Georgian belles heard them, they would have adopted them eagerly.

The important thing was that she captured the insouciance of their period and the flippancy of their verbal expressions, and that she maintained this skill until, with *My Lord John*, she strayed into medieval history, which she researched with her usual diligence but marred with the use of dialogue spiced with unmistakable modern slang, and doubtful medieval phrases on which sharp-eyed critics pounced. The true historical, by such writers as Margaret Irwin for example, would have been researched beyond military or political events of the time; dialectal and idiomatic speech would have been delved into with equal thoroughness and presented accurately.

But when it came to the period novel, Georgette Heyer could never be faulted on any background point. If she said that a stage-coach left The George in Southwark at specific intervals and at specific times, any witch hunter seeking to catch her out would fail. Stage-coach timetables of the period have proved her right every time.

It is logical that if you are obsessed with a particular character in recorded history, royal, political, criminal or any other kind, the urge to use them as a central character will be irresistible. You will research deeply into the biographical details of such characters because they have *lived* and someone, somewhere, may well challenge you about them, besides which you will want your portrayal to be as true as you can make it. For the period novel, on the other hand, since you *create* the characters you will also create their biographical details. This gives the writer of the period novel a big advantage over the writer of the historical.

The genuine historical demands adherence to documented facts. It governs, where the period novel indulges, but at the same time it is not totally restrictive. It can take a slice of recorded history and present it either conventionally or with provocation. It can challenge and even take certain liberties providing it works within the framework of traditionally accepted facts.

This is not to say that a chosen era cannot shackle the 'period' author to some extent, making it difficult and even impossible to change to another. In that event it is useless to try to switch the story to the Georgian, Victorian, Plantagenet, Tudor, Elizabethan or any other period as the case may be. If it needs background atmosphere relevant only to a particular time, your setting and characters must naturally arise from it; beyond that the story is wholly yours.

A classic example of a period novel is *The Mill on the Floss*; of an historical novel depending on dramatic and authenticated historical events, *A Tale of Two Cities*.

Using exotic backgrounds

I am always surprised when people say that a glamorous geographical background (which always means some foreign country) has advantages over a mundane one. For the Mills & Boon type of romance it is probably true, but one has only to think of Catherine Cookson to know that outside such realms it is not. The mundane domestic scene holds its own very successfully.

But if you really want to use an exotic background, don't be discouraged by those who warn you that a particular setting has been 'done to death'. It is true that the *Raj Quartet* and *Far Pavilions* preceded a spate of novels set in India, but the background was not 'done to death' as a result. That happened only to poor imitations. Similarly, Hong Kong has inspired countless novels; so many that the pessimistic warning should have discouraged James Clavell from producing *Noble House*. The success of that alone should demonstrate that if you have a strong feeling for a particular background and passionately want to use it you may certainly do so, but explore it thoroughly first. If you cannot visit it (and even if you can) read everything on which you can lay your hands, but don't think that will be enough if you hope to produce a successful and realistic portrayal.

First you must study the history of the place; read the most comprehensive volume you can find, from cover to cover. One really extensive one will serve you better than several brief or sketchy ones, and when you start to write, keep it beside you for reference. This will prevent you from making mistakes on dates, times, and other historical facts you may use. Then read as many memoirs and biographies as you can of people who have contributed to that history. You may use little or perhaps none of it in your story, but through your awareness of it you will get a greater 'feel' of the place and a sense of identification which will increase as you accumulate the further mass of detail necessary to bring your background to life.

Sociological studies are invaluable and, for other essential facts, travel brochures and travel books can yield useful information on food, shopping, customs, traditions, religious ceremonies and festivities, table and social manners, medical practices, levels of society, immigrant and/or refugee population, currency, sports, train routes, bus routes, taxi fares, markets, and agricultural and horticultural specialities of the region. No facts can be too small or too unimportant to harvest.

You will be wise to get a large and up-to-date wall map of the region, if your story is set in the present day (and by hook or by crook one of the period in which you are writing if the story is set in earlier times). You will also get the latest road maps and street maps and copies of the prevailing motoring laws. Travel brochures will supply you with names and locations of popular stores and restaurants. The Press Offices of appropriate consulates and legations can also prove helpful.

You will also be wise to get some basic grounding in the language of the country, in order to insert correctly spoken sentences when needed – and when you have written your dialogue, do get an authoritative checking.

More novels with foreign settings are written by people who have never been there than readers would ever suspect but, as you can see, it is done the hard way. But nowhere in this book do I say that authorship is easy.

How much of your research to filter into your work is something you will learn instinctively the more you write. If, when reading through the finished story, you sense that you have put in too much, be brave, cut it out and save it for another book. You won't regret it.

Highlighting a scene

Geographical backgrounds, and particularly specific locations, can be used successfully to sharpen an individual scene. By focusing on a well known landmark your reader will see it vividly and the scene will have greater impact. If, for instance, you have chosen London for your setting and you have a dramatic situation, say a showdown between two characters, you can make it more effective by setting it on or by some famous spot, such as Westminster Bridge with the Houses of Parliament towering behind and Big Ben booming the hour while homeward-going crowds push unseeingly by, or cast fleeting glances of curiosity or amusement. The picture will be visually stronger whether the reader is familiar with London or not because such landmarks are world famous.

For comparison, set the scene in an ordinary room in an ordinary house in an ordinary street . . . and see how much more colourful is the first. At such moments, background is your ally. Make the most of it.

A final warning

Before leaving the subject of research, one cautionary note. The fascination of the task can become addictive. The sense of discovery, the excitement of learning the hitherto unknown, can have a mesmeric affect, enticing you on until you can forget what you were looking for initially and be sidetracked into pastures new. There are writers, of whom I am admittedly one, who enjoy research so much that they are easily led astray. So don't be tempted. Be resolute. Remember the job in hand and get on with it.

11
Getting into Print

Preparing your manuscript

Now we get down to the nitty-gritty – marketing your work. The first consideration is the importance of presentation.

Although the word 'manuscript' literally means something written by hand, the word is widely used when referring to an author's typescript. The latter is the professional approach, so never submit hand-written work. No publisher will accept it as final copy. Were you to see some manuscripts that arrive in the 'slush pile' (by which unsolicited work, as opposed to commissioned, is unkindly though not always inaptly known) you would understand why. Most handwritten manuscripts are difficult to read, many almost illegible, and the rest often dog-eared, bearing witness to the fact that they have been going the rounds and meeting with no success.

Even if it is clean and reasonably neat, can you blame publishers or their readers for turning to typescripts which can be read more easily and more quickly, and can therefore expedite a decision? If you don't possess a typewriter, either invest in one (preferably electronic for better results) or, if you can afford it, a word processor because of its many advantages. Since supply and demand have brought prices down many reasonable package deals are available, and bear in mind that self-employment enables you to charge such equipment against tax, also professional charges if you use a secretarial service.

Presentation and layout

Type your story in double spacing on good quality A4 paper, never on flimsy or very thick, and on one side of the sheet only. If you are uncertain, go to a really good office stationer, and ask to see samples of paper suitable for author's manuscripts. It can range from 60 to 80 gsm in weight. 60 gsm is too light, 70 passable, but 75 to 80 is best. I always used 75 gsm until I found a satisfactory 80 gsm which looks and feels like 75 but with additional strength, of a good whiteness, and at a very fair price. Buying a dozen or more reams at a time (500 sheets per ream) is economical.

The old foolscap and quarto sizes have been eclipsed by A4. I have heard it said that quarto should still be used for submission to America, but have never found this to be so.

Use a plain black ribbon and one that is fairly new and therefore not splodgy. A clear typeface can be maintained with a short-bristled brush dipped lightly in methylated spirit, or one of those type-cleaning sheets of stiffened paper, faced with a roughened and magnetic surface, which clean the letters as you type any of the legendary test lines incorporating every letter and digit on the keyboard. Expensive sprays are also available, but for a thorough job the thick, stumpy, well bristled typing brush is best. A new toothbrush will do providing it is strong, and the common pin cannot be beaten for dealing with letters in which dirt can lodge, such as 'a', 'b', 'm', and others with small cavities. Even daisy-wheel printers require occasional cleaning, though far less than the typeface did on the old manual and electric typewriters.

It is highly desirable to maintain a consistent blackness throughout, so change ribbons well before the ink begins to pale. Carbon cassette ribbons for electric and electronic, typewriters, and associated word processors, are excellent; they photocopy well, but have a short life span and are therefore expensive. For anyone who takes a professional pride in the presentation of their work, and can afford them, they are well worth using.

Why is good presentation so important?

Because a clean and clear manuscript saves a lot of time when preparing it for publication. Not only the copy editor appreciates this, but the printer's executive who handles the typesetting. He needs to read the typescript quickly and accurately as he works, at the same time paying attention to a maze of copy editor's and book designer's marks.

The copy editor is the person who 'sees the book to bed', a responsible job which involves considerably more than is imagined by the uninitiated. Checking grammar and punctuation is the very least of his (or her) jobs; he also checks the author's facts, removes inconsistencies and repetitions, suggests re-phrasing badly constructed or ambiguously worded sentences, combs the script for inaccuracies, queries doubtful issues, suggests reshuffling slices if such transitions would improve the book or speed up action or eliminate dragging patches. When your script comes back for approval before going to press (which is always sought by a good copy editor because the book is your creation and your copyright) you may recoil from what appears to be carnage, but after taking a good look you will usually see sense behind it. This is why I say that an author should be grateful for a good copy editor. If you are unlucky enough to get a bad one, you can only pray that his or her editorial days will be numbered.

You can now see why a good typescript is appreciated by everyone involved, how much valuable time it can save, and why your co-operation is worth while.

In America more and more publishers are willing to print direct from an author's word-processing disks, but this means having compatible equipment so that queries and editing can be settled in tandem by 'phone. The practice is not unknown in the U.K. but is by no means prevalent. Such technology is outside the sphere of this book and the immediate subject is how to present your manuscript in an acceptable fashion.

Margins

Wide margins at each side, as well as at head and foot of the page, are important, not only making your script easier to read, but enabling the copy editor to insert instructions to the printer. This is also the reason for double spacing. Small corrections can then be slotted between the lines but, if you do this, write them neatly and clearly, otherwise type them. If you want to insert a good slice of additional copy, retype the page or pages.

For consistency, allow *at least* 1–1½″ at the head and foot of the page, and allocate a fixed number (say 28 to 30) of double spaced lines to the page, including the page number at the top or foot. If word-processed, this will be automatically controlled by parameter settings, and every page will therefore be identical and trouble free. If typing, keep an eye on the lineage and strive to be consistent.

Good margins are also appreciated by the compositor (who sets up the type). He places the page on a stand with side grips to hold them. From this stand he reads your copy, so spreading it too widely leads to difficulties.

Page numbering

One of the assets of word processing is that numbering is done automatically and cannot get out of order or skip a page, though some models, rather irritatingly, don't number the first page of a chapter on the principle that such pages are not numbered in published books; they then proceed to the next page, numbering it correctly but leaving the leading chapter page unnumbered. The nuisance value of this is that if such a page becomes dislodged from the manuscript and is later found, the copy editor (or whoever is currently working on it) has to search through the script to find where it belongs. Scrambling on the floor after an errant piece of paper is bad enough; having to scour a manuscript to find where it should be included is even more tiresome, so if you do invest in a word processor, check whether it can be instructed to number consecutively without a break.

If typing in the ordinary way, make sure you number every page in sequence. Do *not* start a new chapter with a new No. 1. Should pages become misplaced during editing (accidents can happen in the best regulated offices) trying to put chapters in order again, with each one numbered separately, prolongs the task considerably.

Should you repeat a page number in error and therefore have two pages identically numbered (say 331), or if you decide to slot in more copy and need to insert another page (or 'folio', in publishing terms), then label the second one 331A and indicate at the foot of 331 that 331A follows, and at the foot of 331A that 332 follows. Try to avoid doing this too often. It can be as confusing as it sounds.

The title page

Always include a title page. On this print your name and address in the top right hand corner, or your agent's should you be using one. Centre the story's title lower down with the author's name, also centred, a few spaces beneath it. Nearer the foot of the page state what rights you are offering. Should you be submitting it to a magazine, this line should read First British Serial Rights (1st BSR or, as some people put it, FBSR). The sale of 1st BSR permits the magazine or newspaper to serialise the work once, usually prior to book publication, after which the remaining serial rights, including foreign, usually remain with the author though the book publisher may stipulate in the contract that his company takes a percentage of post-publication fees. Certain contractual details are usually negotiable but if you feel strongly on certain points, and have no agent to act for you, don't be afraid to ask for a discussion. Publishers, on the whole, are not ogres. They want to keep their authors (so long as they sell!).

In the case of a short story submission to a magazine, 1st BSR applies to one printing of the story only.

If submitting to a book publisher, you are then offering British Volume Rights (or U.S. Volume Rights if offering in America first). Respective serial rights apply in countries overseas.

Some publishers today seek World Rights and many well established authors find it advantageous to agree but, again, it could be a negotiable point between author and publisher or between publisher and agent. Should you, as a beginner, not have an agent to act for you, seek the help and advice of The Society of Authors regarding any proposed contract, or The Writers' Guild should you be negotiating for a TV or radio script. The addresses of both are included, along with other organisations for writers, at the end of this book.

It is helpful, though not essential, to indicate on the title page the approximate length – or wordage – of your book. If the work has been commissioned, an approximate figure will have been agreed and will be confirmed in the contract, sometimes as 'between 70,000 and 80,000 words' or 'not more than 100,000 words', or, when you reach the enviable heights of well established authorship, length is not stipulated at all. At that stage in your career both you and your publisher will silently agree that the book shall be as long or as short as the story demands, but if you wish to calculate the length the best method of doing so has been issued by publishers Robert Hale Limited. With their consent, I include it below.

> The purpose of calculating the wordage of any typescript is to determine the number of printed pages it will occupy. The precise word count is of no use since it tells nothing about the number of short lines resulting from paragraphing or dialogue (particularly important in fiction).
>
> Calculation is therefore based on the assumption that all printed pages have no paragraph beginnings or endings and the type area is completely filled with words.
>
> To assess the wordage proceed as follows:
>
> 1. Ensure the typewriting is the same throughout in the terms of size, length of line etc. If not, the procedure given below should be followed separately for each individual style of typing and the results added together.
> 2. Count 50 full-length lines and find the average number of words – e.g. 50 lines of 560 words gives an average of 11.2 words.
> 3. Average the number of lines over 10 characteristic pages – e.g. 245 lines on 10 pages gives an average of 24.5 lines.
> 4. Multiply the averages of 2 and 3 to get average per page – e.g. $11.2 \times 24.5 = 274$.
> 5. Ensure the page numbering is consecutive then multiply the word average per page by the number of pages (count short pages at beginnings and ends of chapters as full pages).
> 6. Draw attention to, but do not count, foreword, preface, introduction, bibliography, appendices, index, maps or other line figures.

Finally, repeat your name and address in the bottom right hand corner of the last page.

Despatching the manuscript

Never use paper clips to join chapter pages; they can trap other papers and prove an irritant. Pins can be even worse, as many a red spot on a page can testify. Staples are equally unpopular, necessitating removal by hand (usually with the fingernail!). If packing in a jiffy bag or something similar, secure the bundle of loose pages with strong elastic bands. You can protect them with thin cardboard on top and beneath.

Bound typescripts can be cumbersome and difficult to handle and, in any case, will have to be unbound for despatch to the printer. If you really want to bind the papers, use a loose-ringed binder from which they can be extracted easily.

The best and most acceptable method is to submit the loose pages packed in the box in which the paper was supplied. Not only the printer prefers to handle each folio separately, but so do copy editors and publishers' readers. My long-ago editorial experience taught me this method. Placing the opened box on my desk, and the empty lid beside it, I would then, as I read, put each page face down within the lid until, reaching the end, I would upturn the whole thing and be back at the beginning. I still use this system when checking my own work before despatch.

I also grew to hate carbon copies. If you have ever dealt with smudged and blurred scripts (especially those which have gone the rounds) you will appreciate the discomfort of strained eyes and the abomination of blackened fingers. Send the good, top copy to the publisher and keep a carbon copy for yourself, also a spare one, preferably a good photocopy which neither smudges nor blurs, in case, on acceptance, you are asked to supply a duplicate for the Production Department. You may also be asked to supply one for the cover artist's use. Some publishers stipulate the supply of two manuscripts as a contract clause.

As soon as good, clear photocopying became available, I stopped producing carbon copies of my novels except for my own files. It isn't always cheap but, like stationery and the acquisition of good equipment, it is a business expense and claimable. Public libraries offer photocopying facilities at very reasonable prices. The service is frequently utilised by appreciative authors.

Like word processors, photocopying machines can be purchased for home use. If you have much need of one, it is another worthwhile investment, saving both time and money, but to an author who is not yet launched it will be a luxury until he is writing, and selling, on a steady basis.

G P – two initials to remember

I always maintain that these two letters are, to an author, the most important in the alphabet – and no, they don't stand for General Practitioner but for Grammar and Punctuation. I mention them here because they feature largely when you finally check your completed script. At that stage you must watch for them, lynx-eyed. The same applies to spelling.

I once gave an evening talk to a local writers' circle. When it came to question time I was struck by the persistence of a woman at the back who raised her hand repeatedly despite the spate of questions which, due to an officious 'Madam Chairman' (Chairperson nowadays?), I was obliged to answer as she selected, but I was very aware of the persistent lady and determined she should be given a hearing. It was obvious that she had something to ask which no one else had thought of. To get an unusual question is both a joy and a challenge so eventually, and very determinedly, I forestalled the officious 'Mistress of Ceremonies' and called on that patient lady.

Far from being worth waiting for, her question was a let-down.

'What do you do if you can't spell?'

When I suggested she should work with a dictionary beside her, she replied that it would take up too much time. She added that she 'would have thought it would be the publisher's job to check all spelling anyway'. She also saw no reason why she should bother with grammar and punctuation because 'that should be the copy editor's job, not the author's'. Nor did she appreciate my argument that an author who is being paid to do a professional job should approach it with a professional attitude. As for checking and revising a manuscript until it was as near perfect as she could make it – plainly, she thought me a fusser.

She became more and more truculent until I finally asked how she would feel if a dressmaker she had employed handed over an incomplete garment, saying it would take up too much time to turn up the hem or take out the tackings or do any finishing off, so she could do all that for herself, and still pay the bill. Only then did the questioner subside, very sulkily.

I am not saying that an author is expected to be a perfectionist; what I *am* saying is that it is a good idea to try. None of us is infallible. We all make mistakes. Some of us are good at spelling and others are not, and the same applies to our knowledge of English, but for this very reason any author worth his salt takes a pride in his work and in its presentation. If spelling is not your strong suit, follow my suggestion and work with a dictionary beside you; check doubtful words as you write, or make a note of them and check at the end of your day's stint so you won't forget about them. This method will also save considerable time when checking the complete manuscript before preparing it for submission.

The same applies to grammar and punctuation. I have already commented on the use of adverbs and adjectives, so a brief word now about the split infinitive – that tiresome variation of the infinitive verb which seems to be increasingly prevalent today.

Here is a simple example: 'She started to quickly run across the road.'

In our schooldays it was drummed into us that to split the infinitive (to insert a word or words between *to* and its verb) was a heinous crime, and good copy editors still frown on it. My own aversion is because it often makes a sentence sound awkward. The example should have read: 'She started to run quickly across the road,' which sounds fine, but on the other hand there is such a thing as the justified split infinitive. Of this, C.E. Metcalfe quotes an excellent example: 'We regret it is impossible to legally authorise the termination of the lease.' Correctly written this should be: 'We regret it is impossible to authorise legally the termination of the lease.' But which reads more smoothly? In that instance the split would seem to be justified.

In the interests of a more melodious use of words many people are willing to accept the hitherto unacceptable, but the safest thing is to avoid splitting the infinitive if you can. If you can't, then remodel the sentence.

A particular jarring grammatical mistake, and one which is becoming more widely spread both in speech, in the press, and in literature, is the use of 'different to'. Arguments that it is permissible are blown sky high when countered with 'similar from'.

To avoid such mis-use, repeat in your mind 'different *from*' and 'similar *to*' until, in time, you cease to be guilty of that particular ungrammatical alternative.

Similar errors to avoid are 'try and' for 'try to', 'loan' for 'lend' (*loan* is a noun and *lend* is a verb, but they are commonly confused – eg: 'she loaned me a book' instead of 'she lent me . . .'). Also the use of 'that' in conjunction with an adjective or instead of a simple 'so' . . . 'I was that happy' and 'I was that angry' or 'I don't think he's that clever' should be ' . . . so happy', '. . . so angry', and '. . . so clever.' All such usages can jar when read, even though they pass unnoticed when spoken.

To write grammatically does not mean writing pedantically.

However, grammatical errors can be acceptable and even necessary in dialogue, when such speech can be in character and therefore natural. In narrative, they must be guarded against.

Equal diligence must be applied to punctuation. The omission of correct marks can convey a totally different meaning from that intended. The following paragraph from a Reuter report at the time of the publication of *Hemingway in Cuba* is an object lesson:

> Photos show a young Fidel Castro and an already old Ernest
> Hemingway he was born in 1898 with wide relaxed smiles.

The insertion of omitted parentheses before and after the reference to his birth date will reveal what the paragraph was meant to say. Parentheses can be indicated by brackets, dashes, or commas; in this instance the gaps seem to imply that they were overlooked by the printer. Brackets would have served best although, even then, the construction would have been bad.

If spelling worries you (and even if it doesn't) arm yourself with a good dictionary. The O E D is generally quoted as the authority. If you are uncertain about any aspect of grammar and punctuation, take a day or evening refresher course at your local adult education centre and keep a good book on English grammar and syntax close at hand. Even if you think you don't need it, dip into it now and then and you will discover, not only that it makes fascinating reading, but how much you have forgotten and need to learn again.

Choosing a publisher

Never pick one at random. Check that you are sending your manuscript to one who is likely to consider the type of fiction you have written. It is useless to send a lowbrow romantic novel to a company noted for its highbrow list. It is equally useless to send it, or any other type of novel, to one who publishes only non-fiction. It will merely advertise the fact that you haven't done your homework.

So how *do* you find out publishers' requirements? The first step is to study library shelves for publishers who produce novels of the type you have written. If, however, the publisher of your choice only publishes novels of your particular genre *occasionally*, it can imply that the market there is limited. Very often, librarians are well informed about publishers' lists and helpful with information.

Book shop shelves are well worthy of a study, and a chat with an assistant who really knows his job because he is interested in it (as opposed to the kind who would be equally happy selling peanuts) can yield much useful information.

The reading room of your local library may stock the trade publication, *The Bookseller*; if not, ask for it at the information desk and an obliging librarian will probably let you browse through it on the premises. This publication will keep you up to date with the latest developments in the publishing world; who is publishing what, which books are currently popular and, if you are alert, coming trends. It can be mailed to you weekly. The subscription is high but, again, it can be an investment.

Buy a copy of *Writers' & Artists' Yearbook*. This lists not only United Kingdom publishers and their requirements, but others worldwide. However, because the book is crammed with information of every possible kind covering every possible aspect of writing and publishing, publishers' requirements are inevitably condensed. The *'Yearbook'* is nonetheless a valuable item on every writer's bookshelf, and is reasonably priced.

Another book to consult for publishers' requirements is *The Writer's Handbook* (Macmillan), and there is no reason why you shouldn't write to a publishing house, asking if you can obtain their catalogue. Some still send out copies, despite high production costs.

Submitting your work

Having decided on the publisher whom you would like to publish your fiction, how do you approach him? The simplest way is to send your completed manuscript with a brief covering letter, and await results. This is the method used by many professional authors, letting the book speak for itself rather than submitting a synopsis, or a couple of opening chapters and a synopsis of the remainder, because a story can change substantially in the course of writing. While most publishers make allowances for such changes in the works of established authors, and are therefore not surprised when the story varies from the original conception, it would be foolish for a new author to agree to write a book based on a detailed synopsis, only to finally produce something completely wide of the mark. If, for example, a publisher approved your synopsis of a romantic novel and then you turned it into a piece of crime fiction, you could hardly expect it to be acceptable.

That is why I am not wholly in favour of the submission of opening chapters and a synopsis, a system which is sometimes recommended by tutors and in the pages of magazines for aspiring authors, though in these days of high postal charges such advice is understandable. Packaging and posting a 500-page manuscript, and enclosing postage for its return if unacceptable, can be costly compared with mailing a couple of chapters and a brief synopsis (especially when rejection makes it necessary to send it out again and again), but remember that such costs, along with those of typing paper, ribbons, and other professional expenditure, are an investment authors have to be prepared to make.

It is unlikely that a publisher will commission a novel from an unpublished author on receipt of a couple of opening chapters and a synopsis (what I call a 'partial submission'). One reason is that he must have proof that the author can sustain the impetus of chapters written in the first flush of enthusiasm. This is why he may ask you to submit the complete novel when written, without in any way committing himself to acceptance. All too often a new writer's initial impetus is not maintained, but if the final book does show promise and the possibility that, if licked into shape by an experienced editor, it can be made publishable, it would be an unwise beginner who refused to co-operate.

Chances can be higher for a writer who comes up with a totally new and exciting idea, something no author has ever thought of. Since new plots and new themes and even new backgrounds are notoriously hard to find, it would have to be something really out of the ordinary, something which could be hyped sensationally, and even then it would have to be backed with promising writing, or be produced in conjunction with a more experienced author appointed by the publisher. Such arrangements have been known to launch a new writer on a promising career.

In the face of uncertainty, however, it is wise to complete a book before approaching a publisher. Let us imagine that you have done so and have decided on the one for whose list you deem it to be suitable. First, send a letter of enquiry, but make it brief. Say what the story is about, its theme, and its genre (mystery, suspense, romance, occult, sci-fi, 'straight', or whatever), also approximate length. If the background is a specialised one and you know it well, say so. Then ask if you may submit the manuscript for consideration.

If you can truthfully say that a certain authority has read your book and has advised you to send it on his recommendation, do so if it can be substantiated, but although this might arouse a spark of interest it will avail you nothing if that spark doesn't ignite a similar reaction in the publisher or his professional readers. Don't say that your high-born relatives all declare you to be on a par with Galsworthy or Trollope (why should their birth qualify them as good judges of literature?), or that your friend Mabel adores it, or that you are sure it is right for their list because it is similar to one they recently published (the latter could be a very good reason for rejection!).

Don't be dogmatic: 'This novel is intelligent and well constructed and will interest intelligent people'. Don't be humble: 'I am approaching you diffidently but hopefully . . . '. Don't be flattering: 'I can think of no other publisher who produces books to compare with the excellence of yours'. Don't be patronising: 'I have decided to let you have the chance to publish my work'. And don't be chatty or witty or pally.

Waiting for a decision

How long should you wait? This varies from publisher to publisher, but can be two or three months. This is reasonable; longer is not. Alarming stories are heard about inordinate delays, all of which may be true since publishers do receive a constant flow of manuscripts for consideration, many of which are then sent to outside readers for assessment. In the meantime the poor author waits in a state of tension. Does the silence mean that acceptance is being considered, or does it mean the manuscript is lost? Hope vies with despair, and if no acknowledgement has come to hand (something not unknown, but not excusable) fear takes over.

Because of the uncertainty of mails and the possibility of loss or non-delivery, some authors take the precaution of enclosing stamped addressed postcards along the following (imaginary) lines:

Sender's name and address
Date

It would be appreciated if you would sign and return this card to confirm receipt of the manuscript entitled: *The Desperate Dodo*, by I B Hopeful.

Received on:

Signed:

Publishers:

Someone in the editorial office has only to fill in the blanks and send down to the mailing room, thus saving the publisher the trouble of dictating a letter of acknowledgment and the author a great deal of anxiety. I am told that the percentage of such acknowledgments is high.

If a decision is unduly prolonged, you are justified in enquiring about the current position, but do so politely, either by letter or 'phone. A letter to the Editorial Director is safer than a chat with an underling who promises to 'look into it and call you back', and never does.

Writing a synopsis

If, despite the foregoing, you prefer to send an entire synopsis, a few hints on its construction may be useful.

Writing one about a completed novel is no problem. It is all there before you, waiting to be condensed. Start with brief notes on each chapter, then proceed to an outline of the whole, keeping it as compact as possible.

Writing a synopsis of a book which has not yet been written is a different proposition. It can be unnerving for the reason already touched upon – that many of us have no idea how the story will develop until we are actually writing it, but since you have decided to adopt this method the first thing to bear in mind is that a synopsis is always written in the present tense. (*'Unlocking the door of his office, private eye Dick Jones is confronted with chaos. It has been burgled. He reaches for the 'phone and dials 999.'*).

Ensuing information must be concise because the synopsis must be kept to a minimum. This depends not only on the book's length but on the plot's complexities. A simple romance of 50–60,000 words could produce a synopsis of as little as 700–800, whereas an involved crime novel of 80–100,000 words could require from 1,000 to 1,500. The shorter you can make your synopsis the better. Stick to the bare bones and present your skeleton unadorned.

Protecting your titles

Contrary to the assumption that an author's title cannot be stolen, cases abound which prove otherwise.

I experienced it myself some years ago, when a friend who was branching out from journalism into fiction admired the title of one of my earlier books, originally a magazine serial of which Collins had bought the volume rights. Not a book that mattered much to me, but quite popular in its field.

Some time later she had her first romantic novel published by a rival firm. It bore the same title. Mine was still on the library shelves. My attention was drawn to it by a Chief Librarian who mentioned that he would not be ordering the new *Shadows On The Sand* because duplicated titles confused borrowers and were therefore unpopular. I learned that this decision was likely to be the same elsewhere.

So the person whose sales suffered was the author of the new book, who cheerfully admitted that she had liked the title so much that she had decided to use it and saw no reason why she shouldn't. She was unconcerned about the libraries (there was no P L R in those days) and thought the whole thing 'a bit of a giggle' until discovering that another adverse effect for her was the loss of paperback publication (even though her story resembled mine in no way at all) because a paperback edition of my book was still on the stands. So be warned. Confusion between two books bearing the same title can discourage book-buyers and booksellers as well.

Although she was largely to blame, her publishers were equally so. Titles of books in print can always be checked, and as a precautionary measure it is publishing practice to do so. Titles can be changed at the editorial stage. To do so later is a costly business. Had both author and publisher waited until mine went out of print, they would have been on safe ground.

The truth is that there is no copyright in titles, but there are circumstances in which the use of a title can be restrained. The Society of Authors issues an excellent Quick Guide on the subject and I strongly advise all aspiring authors to get hold of it, along with their other Quick Guides on important aspects of authorship and publishing. They are free to members, but sold to non-members at very modest prices. A list of these guides, which come in a handy booklet form, can be obtained, and copies ordered, direct from the Society. (Address listed under 'Organisations and Societies for Authors' at the end of this book.)

Because the subjects of **Copyright** and **Publishing Contracts** are also too wide and too complex to be covered in detail within this book, I recommend Michael Legat's *An Author's Guide to Publishing* which deals comprehensively and lucidly with both, as well as with many other aspects of publishing that baffle new authors.

Editorial changes

Because the copyright in your book is yours, a publisher cannot alter it without your consent but, as already indicated, a good copy editor can do a lot to improve the books of new authors and I stick by my advice to heed such suggestions, but 'heeding' them does not mean accepting them blindly. You will naturally consider them carefully, summing up whether they really do improve your book. If you think they don't, then say so and point out why. If you feel very strongly about not having a word of your script altered, well, the choice is yours, but I do urge an inexperienced author not to withdraw his book on a wave of indignation because his brain child has been criticized.

I recall being somewhat upset when my son was a small boy and a dentist commented adversely on the way his teeth were growing. I could see nothing wrong with them, but I did have the good sense to heed the dentist's advice for preventive orthodontic treatment, which the poor child endured somewhat uncomfortably for months but later had cause to be thankful for (as I did). So if you can see no flaw in your novel and are somewhat resentful of your editor's comments, take a deep breath and think of the future. Presuming you are sure you have chosen the right publisher, and that you have already signed a contract and cannot therefore withdraw the book without creating ill will or dispute, you will be wise to compromise, and I am confident you won't be sorry.

Not only alterations in construction may be suggested, but changes in incidents to heighten drama or to sharpen a situation, but for the most part these editorial requests will be for cutting, sometimes substantially, sometimes less so, and sometimes because the book is too long and therefore impossible to market at the price which has been carefully assessed for saleability. In the case of the latter, this assessment is usually made before acceptance, and can even be made conditional, so you will have had your chance to refuse at that point.

After acceptance, cutting is usually desirable for the reason already stressed – to improve your novel. This is where you settle down to amicable discussion with your editor, bearing in mind that just as a diamond cutter improves the quality of the stone, so can good cutting improve the quality of a novel. The need for cutting applies to most forms of writing and although the following story (for which I am indebted to my long-standing friend, American author Dean Koontz) applies to journalism, it is nonetheless apt where overwriting is concerned in any field.

The story is traditionally quoted by American teachers of journalism and concerns a news editor who sent an inexperienced reporter to cover a flood in a place called Johnstown. Hours and hours of frustrated waiting passed, and no report came. The editor was frantic when at last it began to come over the teletype, but on and on it went, printing out a melodramatic, ten-thousand-words story unsuited to newspaper reportage and opening with the line: 'God sits tonight in judgment at Johnstown.' Mercifully hanging on to a sense of humour, the editor wired back: 'Forget flood. Interview God.'

No copy editor will ask you to be as drastic as that with your cutting, but the story stresses the need to avoid killing your story with over-writing.

Proof corrections

Not until you receive proofs will you see what your book is going to look like. You will receive two sets, one to be returned when checked and the other for your own use and onto which, if you are wise, you will meticulously copy every alteration you make. Since your novel is there in its entirety, paginated and presented just as it will appear when bound, and since the agreed alterations have been made, you can't see why it should be necessary to check it all through again, but even so you are asked to do so and to return the proofs within a certain time, usually three weeks. It all looks splendid now it is in print, so you skim through it very happily – and shudder, when the final book arrives, to find some glaring printer's error staring you in the face. That error must have been in the proofs, but somehow it went through unnoticed.

It isn't the author's specific job to pick up 'literals' (printer's errors) but you would be wise to keep an eye open for them. It is the easiest thing for them to escape tired editorial eyes (remember that your editor has been dealing with many other books besides yours). One howler which appeared in an American paperback edition of my novel *Dragonmede* leapt out of the first page. The introductory paragraph (quoted in Chapter 8) indicated the mother's scandalous mode of living and because of this the second paragraph began, 'It wasn't surprising that visitors streamed to our tall terraced house in Bloomsbury . . . '. But the 'm' in 'streamed' had been altered to 'k' and this was at a time when streaking in public places was attracting much publicity!

So read your proofs carefully. You will be limited in the amount of alterations you can do at this stage; anything over and above that limit (stated in your contract) will be charged to you because alterations after type has been set are extremely costly. The insertion of one word into a sentence can mean re-setting a whole page and even a whole chapter, an operation no lay person can appreciate. And don't be upset if your single quotes have been altered to double, and vice versa, or the spelling of certain words has been changed, such as those ending in 'ise' (again vice versa). Individual publishers have their own 'house style', sometimes reserving double quotes for quoted extracts or single for lines of dialogue (and yet again, vice versa).

Proof corrections and how to mark them are clearly presented in *Writers' & Artists' Yearbook* and in *The Oxford Dictionary for Writers and Editors*. You will find them fascinating to use.

12
Other Publishing Channels

Literary agents

I had never heard of literary agents until my first day in an editorial office, when I saw a junior sub editor dividing a stack of manuscripts into two piles. One was the slush pile, the other from agents.

Contrary to a wide belief, items from the slush pile were rarely cast aside without a glance, though in many cases one reading of the first page was enough to indicate its quality or suitability. The really dog-eared ones told their own sad tale, as did those with freshly ironed title pages, or sometimes newly typed ones followed by others that needed to be. This taught me the folly of handicapping a story through bad or indifferent presentation.

Very logically, submissions from agents who could be relied on to send something worth considering would have prior consideration, as would those from agents representing established authors.

I soon learned that the time factor also played a part. With four magazines to cater for, the Literary Editor wasted no time in hunting down suitable fiction, so reliable agents were a godsend.

This did not mean that outside submissions were never accepted, for even in a slush pile some undiscovered gem might lie. So exacting was this search for the right fiction that every member of the staff had to read literary submissions in addition to routine editorial work. A really promising writer, whether agented or not, was not often allowed to slip through the net, but fishing in well stocked agency waters invariably yielded a better catch, but if you don't work through an agent, take heart. So long as your work is well presented and your story well constructed, and you are prepared to make changes if requested, the door won't be slammed in your face.

If, when published in magazine or newspaper, you find unexpected alterations, don't be surprised and do try not to be angry. A publication buys first British Serial Rights for one printing only, and so long as the story has not been changed beyond recognition, bear with it. Sometimes a zealous sub editor can overstep the bounds of duty, but in most cases judicious cutting is necessary to fit the story into the requisite space. The alternative may be not to publish at all, so count to three before protesting.

The same applies to the serialisation of a novel. Your real consolation lies in the fact that you *are* published, and in the payment you receive. In the case of well established national publications this will be high, so don't gripe until you are so well established that you can afford to and, even then, remember that there are hundreds of writers waiting to take your place and that no one is indispensable.

Why use an agent?

I know established authors to whom the very word 'agent' is anathema, but they are in the minority and they are usually the rare ones blessed with a faculty for business, which is probably why they begrudge paying ten per cent commission for services they can apparently render for themselves. If you are one of the few creative people with an equal talent for financial wheeling and dealing, and with plenty of spare time in which to make contacts and handle business correspondence and telephoning, then read no further. If you are not, the advantages of having an agent are many.

A good agent knows the state of the market for he is in touch with leading publishers and can therefore keep you in the picture regarding current trends and requirements. He submits your scripts at his own expense, negotiates your contracts, eliminates unfavourable clauses, ensures that the author's rights are preserved, chases dilatory publishers for decisions and negotiates the sale of many subsidiary rights both at home and abroad. He also tries to sell the translation, American and other media rights where possible, often more advantageously than can a publisher who may not have the expertise to exploit such rights. (This does *not* apply to some of the larger publishers who have very experienced rights departments and have close connections with agencies all round the world.) An agent also collects money when due and acts as a merciful buffer between author and publisher should there be any disputes, thereby preventing the relationship from going sour and even preserving friendship between the two parties, who both know that their difference of opinion is solely a business one and not personal (very often difficult to remember when in face to face combat!).

On the other hand, an agent does understand a publisher's problems because many of them have started their careers in publishing. This enables them to explain things which otherwise puzzle authors, to assess whether their complaints are justified, and to tactfully soothe them away.

I have heard it said that an agent forms a barrier between author and publisher, resulting in a lack of personal contact between the two, but this is rarely so, except with a bad agent (and they do exist). The truth is that an agent can, and often is, instrumental in bringing the two together. Through the intermediacy of an agent many a valuable author/publisher relationship has been established.

In reverse, the agent can protect an author from a too-demanding editor, keeping troublesome ones at bay as only an agent knows how. I have had reason to be grateful for this. Alone, could I have begged NOT to be interrupted when a too-persistent editor constantly telephoned to enquire how a work was going, or with ideas for changing it which I knew would not work? Could I, without sounding churlish, have pleaded to be left alone to get on with the job? But a tactful word in their ear, from my agent, left me in peace and goodwill was maintained.

Agency fees

An agent normally charges 10 per cent commission for his services, plus VAT, but a higher percentage on foreign sales. This is because they are made through a co-operating agent resident in the respective overseas country. The foreign agent deducts his commission (usually the same percentage) and forwards the balance to the U.K. agent, who then deducts his own and forwards the rest to the author.

A good agent does not charge a reading fee for manuscripts submitted by would-be clients. Nor does a good agent accept any money until after your book is sold, when he takes his percentage on receipt of the publisher's advance on royalties and on ensuing payments. If he fails to sell your book, he gets nothing, even though he has saved you the cost of postage on repeated submissions and possibly increased his telephone bill on your behalf. Remember that an agent has overheads just as you do, and possibly more; staff salaries, office rent and accompanying costs and services to name a few.

Would an inexperienced author be wise to go to an agent? In my opinion yes, but despite the fact that over 130 United Kingdom literary agents are listed in the *Writers' & Artists' Yearbook* (and the list does not claim to be exhaustive) it may not be easy. Literary agents, as in other forms of trading, exist to sell marketable goods. They have to assess possible profit within a reasonable period, and they will assess you accordingly. If they turn you down, they may be making a mistake, or not. Experienced agents know how to evaluate a manuscript in the light of current publishing trends, and even if your script is not wholly up to scratch they may take a chance on you. Remember that they are in a buyer's market, so can pick and choose. They have to choose well, or fail.

How to find an agent? One way is to study the list featured in *Writers' & Artists' Yearbook*, looking for those with an asterisk beside their name. This indicates that they are members of The Association of Authors' Agents, a professional body to whose standards members are expected to conform. However, this can be misleading since agents are not compelled to join the organisation and several long established and very reputable ones, some of whom existed before the Association was formed, have never done so, so the asterisk does not actually guarantee that only the best and most experienced are amongst its members.

An alternative is to get hold of publishers' catalogues if you can. Some (but not all) publishers indicate the names of literary agents with whom they negotiated individual titles. Count those handled by each agent and then decide whether to approach the agent responsible for the largest number. (His address is almost sure to be in the indispensable *Writer's & Artists' Yearbook*.)

On the other hand, an agent whose name appears beneath only one or two may be an individual operator with a smaller list of clients to whom he can give more personal attention. The catalogue testifies to his ability to sell to a leading publisher so you won't be 'choosing blind' (as some aspiring authors unhappily do) from classified advertisements designed to entice would-be writers to enrol with unheard of agents operating from Little Middleton On The Mud or Much Binding In The Marsh. From choice, go for London agents (nearly all in the Year Book are London-based) for the simple reason that they are situated close to the leading publishers, circulate amongst them, and should have their ears nearer to the ground.

Some major provincial cities have an established quota of agents, mostly concentrating on local markets, but de-centralization from the Capital has not diverted the main core of the publishing or agency worlds.

If you do decide to approach an agent, this is an instance in which it can be wise to submit a synopsis and specimen chapters, accompanied by a brief letter of enquiry. You can indicate the theme of the book or the background (if unusual) and, if you have been published already, include details but, again, briefly. And again, don't make your letter chirpy or chatty, and don't load it with personal information about yourself. At this stage the agent is interested only in your work. *And don't forget to enclose return postage.*

Should you be turned down by the bigger agencies, you will obviously have to focus your sights on lesser known ones, but here again, be careful. A deplorable situation exists in this country (as well as in others) wherein people, with or without agency experience and with little intimate knowledge of the literary world, can set themselves up as literary agents, advertising as such and as 'advisers' and 'literary consultants'. It is a pity that such a situation cannot be legislated against. I was recently told by an author who had just sold her second crime novel to Collins that, in her search for an agent to relieve her of the business side, she met one to whom she had sent a new script and who, in the course of discussion, urged: 'Do send me anything you've written, anything at all, and I'll handle it', only to reveal, after being questioned about the submitted script, that she had not even read it. Wisely, the author took the manuscript home.

Even established agents can vary, some being more competent than others. And there's always the 'one-man's-meat' situation. I once introduced a friend to an agent with whom I was more than content. It proved disastrous. I had not expected their personalities to clash, but they did. If that happens to you, or if you are simply dissatisfied with an agent's services, you are free to go to another. Naturally, you must let the first agent know that you are changing, and he will be entitled to continue acting for you in respect of, and to take commission on, any books he has sold for you if the contracts he drew up have not expired.

Self publishing

The arrival of desk top publishing has enabled authors, whose books have been rejected but who passionately want to see them in print, to produce a limited number of quite acceptable computerized editions, but first they must buy all necessary equipment and then pay for the pages to be stitched (or, if done cheaply, sometimes precariously glued), for a cover to be designed and produced, and finally for the editions to be bound (they must also obtain an ISBN number, which is the only thing to cost nothing). Then follows the crucial problem of promotion and distribution, without which a book can often sink and which can cost considerable time and money.

The computerized system can be useful for producing non-fictional books, or instructional booklets to be marketed by mail order, also to someone wanting to produce a few slim volumes of their poems to give to friends at Christmas, or to raise money for charity, but for fiction it is a different proposition. Fiction is up against the powerful competitiveness of mass market, professional publishers.

A novel needs a strong sales pitch and a well organised distribution team behind it. Good promotion and distribution are costly, and fiction needs these services more than any other type of publishing. And don't forget that, even if your local bookshops did agree to take a copy or two, the booksellers' 30 per cent discount would considerably reduce any profit.

However, if the desire to see your novel in print is so strong that you are prepared to pay accordingly, there are small presses you can employ. (Information can be obtained from the Association of Little Presses, 89a Petherton Road, London, N5 2QT.) There are also concerns which will undertake to handle the whole operation for you, but the lowest printing costs an East Anglian operative (acting as publisher) could obtain for 1,000 copies of a paperbacked book of short stories amounted to £4,000, of which the author paid £3,000. Added to this were other outlays bringing the total to £5,000. The book was nicely produced, but with only two-colour laminated cover (yellow with black printing) it looked rather like a publication from Her Majesty's Stationery Office. Moreover, it contained only 160 pages and had to be marketed at the high price of £9.95.

If your heart is still set on it, get your costing done by an expert. Spearheading the field is the award-winning firm of Scriptmate, whose owner, Ann Kritzinger, got herself and her company into the Guinness Book of Records. Scriptmate Editions are produced to a high professional standard and the company has now advanced from laser printing to the latest digital technology at no increased cost to the self publisher. As few as a dozen copies, in either hardback or paperback, can be produced for testing the market – a huge money saver.

Had the East Anglican enterprise sought a printing quotation from such a source, 1,000 copies of their author's book of short stories, with a two-colour laminated cover, could have been produced for slightly less than £2,500; half of their expenditure. A four-colour cover would have cost slightly more but, even then, would have been far below their outlay. This realistic costing would have enabled the book to be marketed at around £3.95.

When consulted, Ann Kritzinger's advice on the self publishing of fiction was: 'If they want to make a *profit*, my advice to them is "Don't self publish". If they want to test the market and/or have satisfaction and fun, then it's a different matter.'

So consider it carefully. If you have to go out on the road to sell your novel because in addition to your capital outlay you can't afford to employ a skilled representative or marketing service, how much time will you have left in which to write your next one – which, this time, might be accepted by a publisher and prove to be successful? Isn't it better to be paid for writing a book than to pay someone else to produce it? Think about that, and then decide whether self publishing is worthwhile.

Vanity publishing

In no way must self publishing be confused with vanity publishing. The latter is an invidious practice universally condemned in the literary world.

Vanity publishers' advertisements usually run something like this:

AUTHORS – are you looking for a publisher? If your book deserves publication expanding publishers would like to hear from you. Write to:
. . .

That is slightly more subtle than many, and therefore more beguiling. It suggests that they, as publishers, are seeking books which are worth publishing and will consider your manuscript and honestly assess it. In reality, they will accept it however bad it is. Here I quote *Writers' & Artists' Year Book*:

In his efforts to secure business the vanity publisher will usually give exaggerated praise to an author's work and arouse equally unrealistic hopes of its commercial success. The distressing reports we have received from embittered victims of vanity publishers underline the importance of reading extremely carefully the contracts offered by such publishers. Often these will provide for the printing of, say, 2000 copies of the book, usually at a quite exorbitant cost to the author, but will leave the 'publisher' under no obligation to bind more than a very limited number. Frequently, too, the author will be expected to pay the cost of any effective advertising, while the 'publisher' makes little or no effort to promote the distribution and sale of the book. Again, the names and imprints of vanity publishers are well known to literary editors, and their productions therefore are rarely, if ever, reviewed or even noticed in any important periodical. Similarly, such books are hardly ever stocked by the booksellers.

The result of such dealings is that the author is landed with a mass of printed pages and only a few copies of a cheaply jacketed book. He has therefore to hand over more money (if he has any left) to have the loose pages stitched and bound to match those which the vanity publisher has so generously produced, only to find that no one will look at a shoddy product, nor would it be looked at even if well produced because the names of vanity publishers are as widely known to book-sellers as they are to literary editors.

Hopeful authors who have parted with thousands of pounds, and pensioners who have parted with their savings, are by no means unknown. One victimized customer was left with a garage full of unsaleable books and no car because it had been sold to pay the bill. The difference between vanity publishing and self publishing is therefore evident. An author who decides on self publishing knows exactly what he is undertaking. He gets an end product of his choosing, and is prepared to market it as best he can. Self publishing is not a fraudulent proposition. Vanity publishing is, but the skilled wording of their contracts protects these 'literary' pirates.

13
Organisations and Societies for Authors

It is not surprising that writers sometimes wish to escape from the isolation of their work and to seek the company of others similarly employed.

Many clubs and societies fulfil this purpose. Thirty-six pages are devoted to them in *Writers' & Artists' Yearbook*, amongst which the following are but a few:

International P.E.N. is a world association of writers, founded in 1921 under the presidency of John Galsworthy and designed, not only to promote friendship between authors, but to uphold their rights and to promote international good will through the medium of literature. The initials stand for Poets, Playwrights, Editors, Essayists, and Novelists, but membership is open to all writers of standing, including translators, irrespective of sex, creed or race, providing they subscribe to its fundamental principles. Congresses are held in varying countries and individual centres hold regular meetings and literary events. Address of the English centre: 7 Dilke Street, London SW3 4JE.

The Society of Authors was founded in 1884 with the object of representing, assisting, and protecting authors. Its scope includes specialist associations for translators, broadcasters, educational, medical, technical and children's writers. Members are entitled to legal as well as general advice in connection with the marketing of their work, contracts, choice of publisher, etc. Publishes *The Author* quarterly. Address: 84 Drayton Gardens, London SW10 9SB.

The Writers' Guild of Great Britain is affiliated to the TUC and represents writers' interests in film, radio, television, theatre and publishing. Originally the Screenwriters' Guild, the union now includes all areas of freelance writing. Address: 430 Edgware Road, London W2 1EH.

The Society of Women Writers and Journalists hold lectures, monthly lunch-time meeting and workshops, and an annual Weekend School. Publishes *The Woman Journalist* quarterly. Particulars from the Hon. Secretary, Jean Hawkes, 110 Whitehall Road, Chingford, London E4 6DW.

The Crime Writers' Association is for professional writers of crime novels, short stories, plays, and serious works on crime. Associate membership is open to publishers, journalists, and booksellers specialising in crime literature. Publishes *Red Herrings* monthly. Presents several notable awards. Address: PO Box 172, Tring, Herts HP23 3LP.

The Romantic Novelists' Association is open to romantic and historical novelists and presents an annual award for the best romantic novel of the year; also an award for unpublished writers in the same field, who must first join the Association as probationary members. Particulars from the Hon. Secretary, Marie Murray, 9 Hillside Road, Birkdale, Southport, Merseyside PR8 4QB.

The Book Trust (formerly National Book League) exists to foster the growth of a wider and more discriminating interest in books. It organises touring exhibitions and takes part in research projects. It administers many literary prizes and offers members a Book Information Service. *Booknews* is issued quarterly and circulated to members. A Guide to Literary Prizes, Grants and Awards is also available. Its headquarters is a meeting place for members. Address: Book House, 45 East Hill, Wandsworth, London SW18 2QZ.

The **British Science Fiction Association** aims to promote science fiction in all its forms, particularly written, also to provide a forum for discussion, reviews, news and market information. Particulars from the Membership Secretary, Jo Raine, 29 Thornville Road, Harlepool, Cleveland TS26 8EW.

The Authors Club has long been established at 40 Dover Street, London W1X 3RB.

Regional Arts Associations exist to promote and develop the arts, including literature, in their regions. For addresses see *Writers' & Artists' Yearbook*.

Perhaps the easiest way of getting to know fellow writers in your vicinity, both published and unpublished, is through a local writers' circle. The standards of ability and enthusiasm will vary from group to group, but it may be worth your while to find out if there is one within reach. Public libraries usually have details, but a nationwide Directory of Writers' Circles can be obtained from: Mrs Jill Dick, Oldacre, Horderns Park Road, Chapel-en-le-Frith, Derbyshire SK12 6SY.

There are also many residential courses for writers up and down the country. They are very popular, usually moderately priced (according to accommodation and facilities) and offer tuition, workshops, discussion groups and lectures from experts. Prominent among these are the five day courses run by *The Arvon Foundation*, available to people over the age of 16. They are held at two centres based in Yorkshire and

Devon. Details of courses in various fields of writing and related art forms can be obtained from: The Arvon Foundation, Lumb Bank, Heptonstall, Hebden Bridge, West Yorkshire HX6 6DF, or from: The Arvon Foundation, Totleigh Barton, Sheepwash, Beaworthy, Devon EX21 5NS.

A popular and long established **Writers' Summer School** is held at Swanwick in Derbyshire for a week every August. Particulars from: The Writers' Summer School, c/o The Red House, Mardens Hill, Crowborough, East Sussex TN6 1XN.

Many aspiring and practising authors enjoy **Writers' Holidays** at Caerleon College, Gwent, run by the enterprising D.L. Anne Hobbs (30 Pant Road, Newport, Gwent NP9 5PR), and the **Scarborough Writers' Weekend** in April is always well attended. (Write to: Audrey Wilson, 7 Osgodby Close, Osgodby, North Yorkshire YO11 3JW.)

The popularity of the Tunbridge Wells Writers' Weekend is increasing. Founded by the author of this book, it is held each Spring at the luxurious Spa Hotel. Top authors and speakers conduct sessions and workshops in varied spheres of writing. (Write to: The Spa Hotel, Mount Ephraim, Tunbridge Wells, Kent TN4 8XJ.)

There are many more, such as the Southern Writers Conference at Earnley, Chichester, West Sussex; the Scottish Writers' Weekend at Pitlochry; the Southampton Writers Conference at Southampton University, and the *Sunday Times* literary gathering at Hay-on-Wye. All are announced in magazines for writers.

Finally, as soon as you have a book published and know the ISBN number, make sure you register it with the Registrar of Public Lending Right, Bayheath House, Prince Regent Street, Stockton-on-Tees, Cleveland TS18 1DF. This registration will ensure that you receive payments due to you from public library borrowings. Authors owe a great deal to the valiant people who fought for this scheme. To ensure full benefit join the **Author's Lending and Copyright Society** (ALCS), an agency authorised to collect and distribute the moneys. The Society also collects and distributes payments from overseas countries which operate their own PLR system. In addition, the Society is to act as the distribution agency for moneys due to authors under the proposed Copyright Licensing Authority, which will issue licences and collect fees for the photocopying of copyright material. For information write to: The Secretary General, The Authors' Lending and Copyright Society Limited, 430 Edgware Road, London W2 1EH.

Books for authors

Earlier, I advised aspiring authors to build their own 'working' library. Here are a few basic titles from my own bookshelves which will make a good start:

> *The Shorter Oxford English Dictionary* – the standard twelve volume edition condensed into two.
> *The Oxford Dictionary for Writers and Editors*.
> *Roget's Thesaurus* (Penguin).
> *An Author's Guide to Publishing*, Michael Legat, Robert Hale.
> *Writers' & Artists' Yearbook*, A & C Black.
> *The Writer's Handbook*, Macmillan.
> *The Oxford Dictionary of Quotations*.
> *The Oxford Dictionary of English Proverbs*.
> *Brewer's Dictionary of Phrase and Fable*, Cassell. This can be an excellent source for ideas as well as checking facts – and beguiling reading at all times.
> *Research for Writers*, Ann Hoffman, A & C Black.
> *Usage and Abusage*, Eric Partridge, Hamish Hamilton.
> *The Penguin Dictionary of Historical Slang*, Eric Partridge.
> *Modern English Usage*, Fowler, Oxford University Press.
> *Cassell's Classified Quotations*, Gurney Benham. This is easier to find your way around than the Oxford Dictionary of Quotations, being classified under subjects.
> *Encyclopaedia of Superstitions*, Christina Hole, Ed: Radford. Hutchinson.
> *Larousse Encyclopaedia of Modern History*, from 1500 to the present day, Paul Hamlyn. Useful for quick checking, but not for more extensive historical research.
> An up-to-date *Atlas*.
> A *compact* encyclopaedia for handy but not exhaustive reference. For wider research, consult bigger encyclopaedias in your local reference library. The same applies to the *Dictionary of National Biography*, an invaluable source of information.

The above titles will form the nucleus of a *basic* reference library, but you are sure to add to them (the process never ceases). In the meantime they will supplement wider research in specialised libraries. A ticket to the British Library is well worth investing in and a subscription to the London Library, 14 St James's Square, London SW1Y 4LG, is perhaps even more so. This rare library has books which can be found nowhere else and members may take out ten at a time (fifteen for country members, who may also borrow by post but must pay the postage both ways). Subscribers have access to the stacks, the use of a comfortable reading room, and may purchase the printed author catalogue and subject index volumes for home reference; a godsend if you live outside London and wish to order by post or by 'phone.

The staff are extremely helpful. On several occasions they have carefully selected for me a range of titles on specific subjects in response to a telephone call. The subscription may seem high, but for such a service it is not. Short term subscriptions are available. These can be extremely useful if you are on a brief visit to London and want to do some research – and don't forget that such subscriptions, like the purchase of reference books, can be set against a professional writer's tax.

Major provincial cities, also leading cities in Scotland, Wales and Ireland, have libraries equalling those in London, so wherever you live you can be in reach of excellent research sources. The difference between the historic London Library and others is that its incomparable collection of rare books can be matched nowhere else.

Periodicals for authors (mail order)

The Author (quarterly), published by the Society of Authors, 84 Drayton Gardens, London SW10 9SD.

Freelance Writing & Photography (quarterly), published by Weavers Press, Tregeraint House, Zennor, St Ives, Cornwall TR26 3DB.

Writers' Monthly, 18–20 High Road, London N22 6BX.

Writers News (monthly), PO Box 4, Nairn, IV12 4HU.

The Writer (monthly), 120 Boylston Street, Boston, MA 02116-4615, U.S.A.

Bibliography

Agent, Thomas Hinde, Hodder & Stoughton.

Airport, Arthur Hailey, Longman.

The Arrogant Duke, Rona Randall, Collins.

The Assassin, Evelyn Anthony, Hutchinson.

The Boys from Brazil, Ira Levin, Michael Joseph.

Cashelmara, Susan Howatch, Hamish Hamilton.

Catriona, Robert Louis Stevenson, Canongate.

The Conqueror, Georgette Heyer, Heinemann.

The Corn is Green, Emlyn Williams, Samuel French.

Daughter of Time, Josephine Tey, Heinemann.

The Day the Call Came, Thomas Hinde, Hodder & Stoughton.

Death Trap, Ira Levin, Samuel French.

Dragonmede, Rona Randall, Collins.

The Drayton Legacy, Rona Randall, Hamish Hamilton.

The Far Pavilions, M.M. Kaye, Alan Lane.

Frenchman's Creek, Daphne du Maurier, Gollancz.

Gallows Wedding, Rhona Martin, The Bodley Head.

Glenrannoch, Rona Randall, Collins.

Glittering Images, Susan Howatch, Collins.

Goodbye, Mr Chips, James Hilton, Hodder & Stoughton.

The Heyday, Bamber Gascoigne, Cape.

Hotel, Arthur Hailey, Longman.

The Infamous Army, Georgette Heyer, Heinemann.

Jane Eyre, Charlotte Brontë, Dent.

Kidnapped, Robert Louis Stevenson, Canongate.

Looking for Mr Goodbar, Judith Rosner, Cape.

The Malaspega Exit, Evelyn Anthony, Hutchinson.

The Mating Dance, Rona Randall, Hamish Hamilton.

The Model Wife, Nineteenth-century style, Rona Randall, The Herbert Press.

My Cousin Rachel, Daphne du Maurier, Gollancz.

My Lord John, Georgette Heyer, The Bodley Head.

The Mysteries of Udolpho, Ann Radcliffe, Dent.

Madam, Will You Talk?, Mary Stewart, Hodder & Stoughton.

Noble House, James Clavell, Hodder & Stoughton.

The Old Man and the Sea, Ernest Hemingway, Cape.

Pen to Paper, Pamela Frankau, Heinemann.
Penmarric, Susan Howatch, Hamish Hamilton.
The Prime of Miss Jean Brodie, Muriel Spark, Macmillan.
The Raj Quartette, Paul Scott, Heinemann.
Rebecca, Daphne du Maurier, Gollancz.
The Rendezvous, Evelyn Anthony, Hutchinson.
The Rich Are Different, Susan Howatch, Hamish Hamilton.
Rosemary's Baby, Ira Levin, Michael Joseph.
Royal Escape, Georgette Heyer, Heinemann.
The Scapegoat, Daphne du Maurier, Gollancz.
The Stepford Wives, Ira Levin, Michael Joseph.
Strangers, Dean Koontz, Putnam.
The Tamarind Seed, Evelyn Anthony, Hutchinson.
The Wheel of Fortune, Susan Howatch, Hamish Hamilton.
Wide Sargasso Sea, Jean Rhys, Hodder & Stoughton.

Index